PATIENCE FAIRWEATHER

No, You Can't be an Astronaut

Why you shouldn't follow your dreams, and what to do instead

First published by Plausible Press 2023

Copyright © 2023 by Patience Fairweather

All rights reserved. No part of this publication may be reproduced, stored or transmitted in any form or by any means, electronic, mechanical, photocopying, recording, scanning, or otherwise without written permission from the publisher. It is illegal to copy this book, post it to a website, or distribute it by any other means without permission.

Patience Fairweather has no responsibility for the persistence or accuracy of URLs for external or third-party Internet Websites referred to in this publication and does not guarantee that any content on such Websites is, or will remain, accurate or appropriate.

Library of Congress Control Number: 2019950090

Fourth edition

Contents

1	HOUSTON, WE HAVE A PROBLEM	1
2	NOW WHAT?	7
3	IS COLLEGE FOR YOU?	17
4	ALTERNATIVES TO COLLEGE	23
5	SO YOU'RE GOING TO COLLEGE	27
6	ONCE YOU'RE IN, MAKE THE MOST OF IT	37
7	LOOK FOR A JOB	41
8	THE JOB SEARCH	49
9	MAKE YOURSELF FIRE-RESISTANT	65
10	WHAT ABOUT REMOTE WORK?	71
11	A GOOD LIFE, NOT A DREAM JOB	73
REFERENCES		78
FURTHER READING		90
ABOUT THE AUTHOR		91

1

HOUSTON, WE HAVE A PROBLEM

Sasha did everything right.

Right after high school, Sasha went to a big-name research university with Nobel laureates on the faculty. Everyone had heard about the crisis-level shortage of STEM (Science, Technology, Engineering, and Mathematics) majors [1-3], so Sasha chose to major in animal science.

Hoping to graduate in four years, Sasha concentrated on schoolwork and shunned extracurricular activities. Taking on internships [4] and study abroad [5] would have lengthened the time to graduation. Sasha did not know that working at a relevant internship or participating in extracurricular activities during college is associated with around twice the likelihood of being adequately employed after graduation [6]

Sasha never met any of those Nobel laureates on the faculty. They worked mainly with graduate students, it turned out; undergraduates like Sasha never saw them.

After graduating with a decent GPA, Sasha expected to earn enough to pay off student loans quickly. Unfortunately, competition for the few desirable jobs was fierce, and many vacant positions were in remote areas. They offered no moving allowance or job security, and the pay was disappointingly low. Sasha's situation wasn't unique; although most of Sasha's classmates found work, half of them were in jobs that didn't require a college degree at all [7].

After a few months of job-hunting, Sasha now works a part-time job.

Working hours are limited so the employer can avoid paying benefits. Sasha's unpredictable on-call work schedule makes it nearly impossible to go back to school for an advanced degree [8] Online education is a possibility, but degrees earned online aren't as well-respected as their traditional face-to-face counterparts [9]. Fortunately, Sasha has health insurance, courtesy of Mom and Dad...at least for now.

Sasha's story is not unusual. Although only four percent of recent college graduates are unemployed, an additional 39 percent work in jobs that typically don't require a college degree. And it's not just the much-maligned performing arts (70% underemployed) or ethnic studies (48% underemployed) majors who are taking your coffee order or folding shirts at the mall. 71% of criminal justice majors and 56% of business management majors are working in positions that typically don't require a college degree [7].

Unfortunately, despite pundits and business leaders trumpeting the need for more STEM graduates [10], it turns out there isn't really a dearth of STEM workers after all. The "shortage" appears to be not one of qualified workers, but of workers pre-trained in specific specialties who are willing to accept the salaries on offer [11, 12]. Schools in the U.S. churn out more STEM graduates than there are available jobs, leading to oversupply in some fields [2, 3, 13].

HOW DID WE GET HERE?

The college degree used to be rare. In 1950, only six percent of U.S. adults over 25 had a four-year degree or higher. It was a credential that really stood out. But today, 38 percent of U.S. adults over 25 have a four-year degree or higher. The college degree today is more common than a high school diploma was in 1950 (38% vs. 34%) [14].

Supporters of increased rates of college degree attainment cite the fact that people with college degrees earn more, on average, than people without them [15]. The assumption is then made that increasing the number of college graduates will increase the number of people earning high wages [16, 17]. This rests on two assumptions:

1) The demand for college graduates will rise to meet the supply, and

2) There are, or will be, enough "good" (high-paying, stable) jobs out there to absorb the increased output of college graduates.

The first assumption is correct. Given a choice between two similar applicants, employers generally will hire the more-educated candidate. As the supply of college graduates has increased, companies have increased their hiring of college graduates for jobs that used to require only a high school diploma, and of graduate degree holders into positions requiring a bachelor's degree [18]. As college graduates fill the jobs that high school graduates used to get, high school graduates are left with fewer opportunities [19]. The worsening outcomes for those with only a high school education [20] appears to be the source of the "College Premium."

Claims of an undersupply of college graduates are at odds with the evidence. Increasing the number of college graduates has not coincided with an increase in good jobs for those graduates; in fact, the opposite has happened. Since 1980 average income has decreased, the number of poverty-wage jobs has grown, and the percentage of jobs that are temporary or on-call has gone up [21]. A much-cited 2010 Lumina Foundation study, *Help Wanted: Projections of Jobs and Education Requirements through 2018*, projected that by 2018, 33% of all job openings would require a bachelor's degree or higher, while an additional 30% would require some post-secondary education [17]. While the Department of Labor projects that jobs requiring some post-secondary credential are projected to grow faster than average, as of 2022 only 24% of jobs in the United States currently require a bachelor's degree. (Recall that 38 percent of U.S. adults over 25 have a four-year degree or higher). An additional 11% require an associate's degree, certificate, or some college. 60% of jobs require only a high school diploma or no formal credential [22].

U.S. employers aren't offering more good jobs to accommodate the increased number of college graduates; instead, they're requiring college degrees for the jobs that used to go to high school grads [23].

Low-wage and part-time jobs are increasing as a percentage of total jobs [24]. The defining problem in the U.S. job market isn't a skills gap; it's that too many educated people are chasing too few jobs [18] while employers offer less training and less job security [1]. As education levels have increased, the poor have simply become better-educated [25].

How did the authors of *Help Wanted* predict a need for more college degrees when it was already clear that college graduates outnumbered suitable jobs? By assuming underemployment doesn't exist. They define the size of the college labor market as a function of the number of college graduates currently employed in a given occupation [26]. For example, if 15% of taxi drivers have bachelor's degrees [27], that means 15% of taxi driver jobs need bachelor's degrees [26].

The Center on Education and the Workforce is funded by the Lumina Foundation for Education [28-30] which has roots in the student-loan industry. When the nation's largest administrator of private student loans sold its assets to Sallie Mae, the Lumina Foundation was created with the proceeds, and former Sallie Mae board members have served as directors of Lumina [31]. The Lumina Foundation's stated goal is "increasing the proportion of Americans with high-quality degrees, certificates and other credentials to 60 percent by 2025" [30]. Considering this history, Lumina's relentless efforts to increase college enrollment could be seen as a conflict of interest.

But the college completion agenda is appealing even to those without ties to the student loan industry. Increased college attainment is a simple, feel-good goal that allows advocates to ignore thorny structural issues around the worldwide labor market [32].

WHEN A COLLEGE EDUCATION IS NO LONGER RARE, IS IT STILL VALUABLE?

College degrees in the job market behave like a positional good [33]. A positional good is something that is valuable because it is scarce—the more people have it, the less it's worth [34].

Individually, chances are you're better off with a degree than without one (on average; results vary [35]). But collectively, the more people earn college degrees, the less likely the average graduate is to attain a "good" job [36].

Although college can be expensive, and graduates often end up in jobs that do not require college degrees, there is a practical reason to pursue a degree: While the rewards for a degree are diminishing, the penalty for not having one is increasing. Employers use the four-year degree as an easy way to filter incoming applications [37].

WHY DIDN'T ANYONE TELL ME HOW HARD IT IS TO FIND A GOOD JOB?

Your counselors probably never told you that we have an oversupply of educated job seekers. That's probably because no one told them. On the contrary, the career-advice industry is brimming with positivity. There's no shortage of books, inspirational posters, and desk plaques claiming that you that with the right attitude you can get paid for doing what you love. Why settle for a mere job, the gift-shop gurus ask, when you can follow your calling and fulfill your destiny?

The advice to "follow your dreams" is meant to be encouraging, and for some people it may be. But what if you don't have a particular passion that you yearn to pursue twenty hours a day? Are you a bad person if you actually do look forward to Fridays more than you look forward to Mondays?

WHAT'S WRONG WITH FOLLOWING YOUR PASSION?

Following your passion is fine—as long as you don't expect to get paid for it. Because as individual and unique as you undoubtedly are, your "passion" is probably the same as a lot of other people's. As life coach Gabrielle Loehr observes, "not everyone's passion can turn into a paying job and your bills are not going to pay themselves [38]." Here are the numbers: Most professional writers earn less than a thousand dollars a year from their writing [39]. Few aspiring athletes ever end up playing professionally [40]; for basketball players the odds are less than one in 10,000 [41]. And astronauts? NASA takes fewer than 1% of applicants [42, 43]. If you're an MBA, your probability of ending up as a CEO is less than a 0.001% [44].

NO, YOU CAN'T BE AN ASTRONAUT

More of this at www.onlinecasino.ca/odds-of-success/

2

NOW WHAT?

In the previous chapter you learned that there aren't enough good jobs to go around, that employers are paying less and expecting more, and that you're more likely to get struck by lightning than to achieve your dream career.

But there's some good news too (really). It will take planning, persistence, and flexibility, but you can launch a career that fits your interests and abilities. In the following pages you will get an overview of the latest research in organizations and careers, complete some useful self-assessments, and discover the array of employment and educational opportunities available to you.

WHAT ARE YOUR INTERESTS?

There is a grain of truth in the advice to "follow your passion," and it is this: People whose work fits their interests and preferences tend to be on average slightly happier in their jobs [45, 46]. It's risky to bet everything on a high-stakes dream job. But it's smart to figure out in advance how much you enjoy (or can tolerate) working with your hands, interacting with people, manipulating numbers, or following a routine.

Realistic, Investigative, Artistic, Social, Enterprising, or Conventional?

The RIASEC typology describes to what extent you would be comfortable in Realistic, Investigative, Artistic, Social, Enterprising, or Conventional jobs.

Realistic occupations are hands-on, practical, and often physical. Examples are forest ranger, auto mechanic, and quality control inspector.

Investigative occupations involve analyzing information and working in the realm of the theoretical. Investigative occupations include college professor, mathematician, and computer programmer.

Artistic occupations are intuitive and creative. This category contains dream jobs like photographer, illustrator, and musician. It is sometimes said that these are called "dream jobs" because if you think you can pay your bills with them, you're dreaming. But Artistic types can make a decent living by helping other Artistic types pursue their dreams. For example, photographer Tony Northrup has several bestselling books on photography and photo enhancement software; musician Joseph Alexander has sold over 200,000 copies of his manuals on guitar technique; and one of mystery author Nancy J. Cohen's bestselling books is Writing the Cozy Mystery, an instructional book for aspiring mystery authors.

Social types are energized by working with people and helping them to solve their problems. Occupations in this category include counselor, social worker, and elementary school teacher. Social careers tend to be those that benefit society and help the young and the vulnerable, so they are not very well paid.

Enterprising occupations are those that involve managing, persuading, and making money. Sales, politics, and management careers fall into the enterprising category. These jobs tend to be well paid, and are suitable for thick-skinned extroverts.

Conventional careers are practical and predictable, and best suited to the conscientious and the patient. Conventional occupations include accountant, financial analyst, and IRS agent.

To find your RIASEC type, access The O*Net Interest Profiler, sponsored by the U.S. Department of Labor, at **mynextmove.org/explore/ip**.

Once you have your RIASEC interest profile, you can browse careers compatible with your interests at **onetonline.org/find/descriptor/browse/1.B.1**.

WHAT CAN YOU OFFER?

The RIASEC framework is focused on what you want from a job; to clarify what you can offer an employer, visit careeronestop.org/Toolkit/Skills/ . Here you can access skill assessments for career starters, career changers, and veterans. These tools help you translate skills you've developed into terms that employers understand and value.

EMOTIONAL INTELLIGENCE

Emotional intelligence (EI) is the ability to know and manage your own feelings, and to sense and react appropriately to the feelings of others. EI is a strong predictor of workplace success [47-49]. This isn't surprising, when you think about it. You need to be able to sense the mood of your manager, customer, or co-workers, and to respond appropriately. You should also be able to exercise self-control and avoid emotional outbursts in the workplace.

How emotionally intelligent are you?

One well-known measure of emotional intelligence is the Mind in the Eyes test [50]. The MITE test requires you to read emotions based on a photo of a person's eyes.

You might think it would be difficult to read emotions from a black-and-white photograph of someone's eyes, but you may be surprised at how many items you get right. You can try the Mind in the Eyes for yourself at socialintelligence.labinthewild.org/mite/.

The original MITE test has been criticized for using only European-looking faces (the photographs are taken from 1990s British magazines) and gender stereotyped "correct" answers. In addition, because photographs were taken from magazines, the "correct" answers on the MITE do not necessarily reflect what the person in the photograph was actually thinking or feeling.

Researchers are currently working on the Multiracial Reading the Mind in the Eyes Test, an updated test that addresses these concerns [51] but it is not yet widely available.

Another test of the ability to discern others' thoughts is the Personality-Based Emotional Intelligence Test, which asks you to infer the motivations behind people's statements [52]. You can take this test online at openpsychometrics.org/tests/EI.php.

The above tests are "ability based." The test-taker is asked to make judgments about what someone else is thinking or feeling and the answers are either right or wrong. Another kind of assessment is the self-report instrument. Self-report instruments ask test-takers to evaluate their own skills. Other-report instruments are used to get feedback from others [53]. In the next section we will use self-report and other-report methods.

Improving your emotional intelligence

We are very bad at judging our own interpersonal skills. Muriel Maignan Wilkins writes,

"In my ten years as an executive coach, I have never had someone raise his hand and declare that he needs to work on his emotional intelligence. Yet I can't count the number of times I've heard from people that the one thing their colleague needs to work on is emotional intelligence. This is the problem: those who most need to develop it are the ones who least realize it." [54]

If you have accepted that your interpersonal skills might need some work, congratulations—you're already ahead of a lot of other people!

It is possible to improve your emotional intelligence. Emotional Intelligence appears to be related to physical brain function [55], but your brain is not unchangeable. Insufficient sleep, for example, can temporarily reduce your emotional intelligence [56]. In addition to getting enough sleep, you can improve your EI through training and practice. Training that focuses on interpersonal and conflict resolution skills has been shown to improve leaders' management skills, leading to happier employees and higher productivity[57, 58].

Executive coaching in particular has been shown to be effective in increasing leaders' emotional intelligence [58], but this approach can be expensive and time-consuming. Fortunately, there's a do-it-yourself solution. It will take a little effort, a lot of humility, and a few patient acquaintances.

Your DIY Executive Coaching Program

This method depends on getting people's candid assessments of your interpersonal skills. If you are fortunate enough to have two or three people who are willing to help you, here's what to do next.

- Recruit your coaches: friends, family members, teachers, and counselors to help you with this. Choose people who get along well with others and are therefore likely to have high emotional intelligence.
- Promise them you will not get mad at them.
- Ask them to complete the following five-item questionnaire on your behalf [52]:

1. Self-awareness is the ability to observe yourself and recognize your feelings as they occur. How self-aware is_____?

. 2. Managing emotions means handling both negative and positive emotions well. How good is _____ at this?

. 3. Self-motivation includes controlling emotions to reach a goal, delaying gratification, and ignoring distractions. How self-motivated is _____?

4. Empathy is sensitivity to others' feelings and concerns, the willingness to see things from another's perspective, and acceptance of the differences in how people feel about and react to things. How empathetic is_____?

5. Handling relationships involves perceiving and managing emotions in others and displaying social competence and social skills. How is _____ at managing relationships?

- Fill one out about yourself.
- Collect all the assessments. Thank everyone for their time and effort.
- Compare. Is your assessment of yourself very different from others' assessments? If four people who know you have rated you as not very perceptive of others' feelings, while you have rated yourself exceedingly high, you should consider the possibility that you're not as perceptive as you might believe.
- Remember your promise not to get mad at anyone. Show appreciation, even if you are offended by the feedback. Don't forget, you asked them to do this, and they took the time and effort to comply! Consider sending a handwritten note or email along these lines:

Dear [Name],

I want to express my heartfelt thanks for taking the time to fill out the emotional intelligence questionnaire on my behalf. Your willingness to help me out means so much to me, and I truly appreciate your support.

Sincerely,

[Your Name]

- Now you are armed with some knowledge and perspective. You have a good idea of how others see you, and where your self-image might be at odds with that. It's time to act.
- Practice observing your own feelings in a detached and unemotional way. This is something that people who are high in emotional intelligence do naturally. Their emotion and their self-reflection operate independently. They can step back and observe themselves.
- People with low emotional intelligence have their emotions all tangled up with their other mental processes [55]. Do your best to step back and "untangle" when you can. For example, if you are feeling annoyed, ask yourself, **why am I feeling this way?** Does this barista/ cashier/ driver really deserve my wrath? Or am I feeling angry because I experienced other annoyances today, and this person crossed my path at the wrong time?

- Practice taking responsibility for your feelings and your behavior. Yes, there are people out there who are mean, or incompetent, or infuriating. And they can frustrate and upset you. Recognize and acknowledge those emotions. They are normal. But these feelings don't give you the right to make other people suffer. You don't have to yell, hit people, or say or do things that will destroy relationships or careers.
- Practice empathizing. **Try to imagine what it's like to be someone else** and observe the world through their eyes. The braggart, the know-it-all, or the undermine-y friend can be annoying. You may be tempted to put them in their place. But think about why they are acting this way. They may be insecure, so challenging their already-fragile self-esteem will only make things worse. Or they may be eager to share their knowledge, and unaware that they are dismissing other points of view. Is it so important to set them straight?
- Accept that **this is a lifelong process**. The more you work on it, the more you'll improve.

PERSONALITY

There are many ways to measure aspects of your personality. The Myers-Briggs Type Indicator and the Big Five are two of the most popular and well-known.

The Myers-Briggs Type Indicator

The Myers-Briggs Type Indicator (MBTI) is popular and widely used in high schools, universities, and human resources departments. However, it is not intended to be used for job placement:

"The MBTI® assessment is not intended for use in selection of job candidates, nor for making internal decisions regarding job placement, selection for teams or task forces, or other similar activities. The Myers & Briggs Foundation is clear regarding the ethical use of the MBTI assessment: It is unethical to require job applicants to take the assessment if the results will be used to screen out applicants." See themyersbriggs.com/en-US/Support/MBTI-Facts for more on this.

The instrument is intended to help people understand each other and to aid in self-reflection. The MBTI measures these four preferences:

Extraversion vs. Introversion. Do you get your energy from being around people, or do you need alone time?

Intuition vs. Sensing. Do you think in abstract terms and see connections others don't, or do you feel more comfortable with the useful and the practical?

Thinking vs. Feeling. Do you make decisions based on facts and logic, or your feelings and values?

Judging vs. Perceiving. Do you prefer structure and schedules, or flexibility [59]?

The Myers-Briggs Type Indicator is the intellectual property of the Myers & Briggs Foundation. The Foundation makes the official MBTI is available online for a fee at mbtionline.com/en-US/Products/For-you.

There are free sites with tests that approximate the MBTI. Sites offering free tests include:

truity.com/page/16-personality-types-myers-briggs

humanmetrics.com/cgi-win/jtypes2.asp

16personalities.com/free-personality-test

Although it is popular in corporate and counselling settings [60], the MBTI is not held in universally high regard among personality researchers [61, 62]. A competing personality framework, the Big Five [63], has been tested and validated in a number of contexts and is more widely used in psychological research.

The Big Five

Research has shown that personalities vary along five main dimensions. These are known as the Big Five or O.C.E.A.N. (Openness, Conscientiousness, Extraversion, Agreeableness, Neuroticism) dimensions.

Openness to Experience covers intellect, imagination, and independence.

Conscientiousness is responsibility and dependability.

Extraversion characterizes someone who is talkative, assertive, and energetic.

Agreeableness describes someone who is trusting, good-natured, and cooperative.

Neuroticism is the opposite of calm and emotional stability.

Remember the RIASEC career interests? They line up with the Big Five personality dimensions as you might expect them to. Artistic and Investigative types are high in Openness. Enterprising types tend to be extroverted, while those with Social interests are both extroverted and agreeable [64].

The Big Five has never been as popular as the Myers-Briggs Type Inventory (MBTI), even though the Big Five has more research supporting its usefulness in the workplace [65, 66]. This may be partly because the MBTI was developed and commercialized by two dedicated individuals [67]while the Big Five / O.C.E.A.N. framework emerged from academic research [68]. The MBTI has the added advantage of being unlikely to hurt anyone's feelings. No matter which MBTI type you are, you can find something positive to say about it. Are you an ISTJ? According to the MBTI, you can be stubborn and insensitive, but you are also responsible and honest. An ENFP diagnosis marks you as emotional and impractical, but also charismatic and creative. Each type has its advantages and disadvantages, and its own place in an organization [69]. A Big Five assessment, on the other hand, might describe you as unimaginative, neurotic, disagreeable, or lacking in conscientiousness. Who wants to hear that?

But even the Big Five characteristics have unexpected advantages and disadvantages, depending on one's situation and occupation. Openness to experience tends to be correlated with high academic achievement and verbal ability, so you might think that higher scores on this dimension are always better. But people with very high levels of openness to experience might not do well in jobs that require memorization or attention to detail [70].

Those high in neuroticism tend to be less satisfied with their jobs and their lives than others. However, neurotic or emotionally unstable people are more prevalent in creative occupations, and this trait can be helpful in generating new ideas. Neuroticism combined with high conscientiousness is associated with better health [71, 72]. The tendency to worry appears to be associated with high workplace performance when combined with high intelligence [73].

Agreeableness helps you to work well in a team, but being too agreeable may work against a leader. Jobs that require you to disagree with or thwart others (labor negotiator, nightclub bouncer, police officer) require a certain level of disagreeableness.

Conscientiousness is a strong predictor of workplace performance [74-76], but even this valued trait can have a downside. Conscientious people may not handle stress and setbacks as well as others. They experience lower well-being after unemployment [77] and may have a stronger fight-or-flight response in stressful situations [78].

You can take a Big Five test online and have it scored automatically here: openpsychometrics.org/tests/IPIP-BFFM/

A newer variant on the O.C.E.A.N. model is the six-factor HEXACO, which adds Honesty-Humility as a sixth factor. You can take the HEXACO Personality Inventory at hexaco.org/hexaco-online.

Risk Tolerance

Are you willing to bet everything on getting your dream job, or would you rather work toward an attainable career goal? The Goal Motivation and Risk Tolerance Test will help you think this through. You can take it here: psychologia.co/goal-motivation-and-risk-tolerance-test

Now that you have some insight into your personality and preferences, let's look at your next steps.

3

IS COLLEGE FOR YOU?

Should you go to college? More specifically, should you go now?
   It depends.

WHAT DO YOU WANT FROM COLLEGE?

If you want a lucrative career, keep in mind that the most secure occupations tend to be those where you manage people, manage data, or manage money. Attending a brand-name school is great if you have the opportunity, but for undergraduate degrees, your major might be more important than your alma mater. A business major from a top university will earn more than a business major from a non-selective university; but the business major from a non-selective university will earn more than an education major from a top university [79-81]. If you think business and engineering are boring and you want to follow your passion for early childhood education or counseling psychology, make sure you can afford it.

If you have your heart set on a particular school, don't be afraid to network. Spread the word that you are interested, and you might find that someone you know has a connection to your dream school. A good recommendation from a booster, faculty member or former student can make a difference.

HOW MUCH WILL YOU NEED TO EARN?

It can be eye-opening to discover how much you need to make to support the lifestyle you want. If you are happy living with a roommate in an inexpensive city with no children, few luxuries, and no vacations, you will have more career possibilities open to you.

Take this quiz to see what you need to earn to support your desired lifestyle. This interactive worksheet is designed for entry-level jobs. Whether you plan to attend college now, later, or never, it's helpful to know what you will need to earn to support the lifestyle you want.

jumpstart.org/what-we-do/support-financial-education/reality-check/

College graduates have higher salaries and lower unemployment rates than non-graduates. Graduates also enjoy better mental and physical health, better exercise habits, higher rates of voting and volunteering, and longer lives [82-84]. Policymakers and parents, after seeing this information, could hardly be blamed for encouraging high school graduates to go to college.

But as we saw earlier, the more college degrees are awarded, the less valuable they are in the labor market. Pumping more college graduates into the economy doesn't magically make more jobs spring up to meet them [36, 85]. As educational attainment has increased in the United States, so has the proportion of poor people with degrees [25, 86]. Around ten percent of the people living in poverty today in the United States have bachelor's degrees or higher, and around five percent of people with bachelor's degrees or higher live in poverty [25]

Simply comparing the outcomes of graduates and non-graduates doesn't reveal *why* college graduates have better job outcomes. Do universities simply select people who would make good employees and filter out those who wouldn't? Or would a given individual do better in life with a college degree than without one? It's **impossible to run a truly randomized experiment in an ethical way**. Two *un*ethical ways you could answer this question would be to either (a) find a group of college-bound students and randomly bar half of them from higher education, or (b) take a group of non-degree-holders and randomly award half of them degrees from a reputable university.

It's unlikely that either of those studies will be done, so researchers do their best to work around their limitations. They might compare students who are just above or below a cut-off point, or use detailed survey data to try to adjust for selection bias.

The studies that have been done suggest that *on average* the college degree pays for itself eventually, and *on average* some college is better than no college [35, 87, 88].

However, keep in mind that individual results vary. There is no guarantee that you will attain the "average" outcome.

MAJOR MATTERS

The areas of study that lead to the best-paid jobs are concentrated in engineering, computer science, business, and health care [75, 76]. By contrast, the earning power of a completed arts or humanities degree is equivalent to not finishing college. Those who go into debt for an expensive arts degree will, on average, not break even in their lifetimes [35, 89].

But averages hide a lot of variation, and people often attend college for reasons other than making money.

IF YOU START COLLEGE, WHAT'S THE CHANCE YOU'LL FINISH?

To see the probability of someone with your characteristics graduating in 4, 5, and 6 years, see HERI's Graduation Rate Calculator, based on over 200,000 first-time, full-time college students:heri.ucla.edu/graduation-calculator/. Keep in mind that predictions like this work well on the aggregate level, but not on the individual level. We know that around half of students with ACT scores of 30 and high school GPAs of 3.2 will graduate within four years, but we don't know *which* half.

With these cautions in mind, your probability of completing college is higher if these apply to you [90]:

- You were reading by the 3rd grade
- You were absent less than 10% of the time in high school
- You failed no more than one class in ninth grade
- You took college classes in high school
- You did a summer bridge program
- You completed calculus in high school

Even for those who complete college, the lifetime returns to a four-year college degree can vary. Higher education is not exactly a great equalizer: those from low-income backgrounds have a return to a college degree of up to $500,000 (which is not too bad), while the college premium for graduates from high-income backgrounds is close to $1.4 million. The best-paying jobs accrue to those who are already more advantaged:

"Individuals who earn a graduate degree, are white or male, or come from a family with income above 400 percent of the poverty line, are much more likely to achieve very high earnings than similar individuals from a low-income family... whose earnings boost from college is particularly small [91:27]."

Is it ever not worth it to go to college? Personally, I believe that education has value in itself, and that the knowledge and critical thinking tools acquired in the course of a college education make life more meaningful and enjoyable. In addition, having some college is better, *on average*, than no college at all [88]. However, college doesn't pay off financially for everyone [35, 36, 92].

WHAT IF YOUR CHANCES DON'T LOOK GOOD?

Suppose you've estimated that your chances of graduating from college are low, but you still want to go. We already know that a low-cost institution gives you the best chance of a positive return on investment [35]. What else can you do to maximize your chances of your college degree paying off for you?

Start at a community college

Community colleges offer small classes, low prices, and a focus on teaching. Taking your first two years of coursework at a community college is a great way to save money and get more personalized instruction. Many universities will accept a two-year degree from a community college and count it toward two years of a four-year degree. Make sure to talk to a counselor or academic advisor about which classes to take if you plan on transferring to a four-year school.

Choose a teaching-focused four-year school

If you want to avoid getting lost in the crowd, choose a school where undergraduate education is the top priority. These are generally not the schools that are famous for their high-profile scholars or their winning football teams.

How can you tell whether undergraduate education is a priority?

Typically, an undergraduate-focused school will say their mission is based on Liberal Arts or a Liberal Education. These schools don't need to be expensive; check out the Council of Public Liberal Arts Colleges at coplac.org. The term "liberal arts" refers to the traditional disciplines in a university: arts and sciences, as opposed to vocational education. A liberal arts –focused university has come to mean one that is mostly residential, emphasizes experimentation and intellectual growth, and represents undergraduate education at its best [93].

Research-oriented universities tend to be high-profile and highly selective. As their name implies, they are focused on producing research, not on teaching undergraduates. Visit carnegieclassifications.iu.edu/lookup/lookup.php and look up the university you're considering. If you see the classification Doctoral Universities: Highest Research Activity, you may want to reconsider attending as an undergraduate. A research university is a great place to go for graduate school. But undergraduate education is not prioritized or rewarded at R1 institutions [94], and a struggling undergraduate student is not likely to get a lot of support.

Once you have selected a few schools of interest, see whether you can talk to someone in their admission office. (If you can't get anyone to talk to you or call you back, you may want to cross the school off your list. If they ignore you now, when they're supposedly trying to woo you, imagine how much worse it will be once you're already a student!) Ask what percentage of classes have fewer than 20 students (according to some research, the best size for student success and persistence) and what percentage enroll more than 50 [95-101].

Ask what kinds of support programs you can join. Many schools have programs for first-generation, low-income, or other groups. Some schools offer summer bridge programs for the transition from high school to college; these can be extremely helpful.

AVOID FOR-PROFIT SCHOOLS

For-profit institutions exist to funnel student loan money into their investors' pockets, and they are very good at that. Graduates of for-profits earn no more than high school graduates, and in some cases the relationship to earnings is negative. Students who attend for-profits have more debt, higher rates of default, and worse job market outcomes compared to those who attend nonprofit schools [102, 103]. While there are some good people who work at for-profit institutions, they are set up to benefit investors, not students. To find whether a school is for-profit, search for it at collegescorecard.ed.gov or carnegieclassifications.iu.edu. The search results will include whether the school is for-profit or non-profit.

4

ALTERNATIVES TO COLLEGE

If you decide to forego a college degree, you're not alone. Two-thirds of American adults don't have four-year degrees, and the high school diploma is still the most common entry-level credential [14].

CONSIDER A "DIRTY JOB"

Mike Rowe of "Dirty Jobs" fame has started a foundation to promote and support vocational arts education and the trades. He points out that while more and more high school graduates are heading to college, most jobs don't require a college degree: "We keep lending money we don't have to people who can't pay it back for jobs that don't exist." The website has an active jobs listing page at jobs.mikeroweworks.org.

EXPLORE OCCUPATIONS AT THE BUREAU OF LABOR STATISTICS

The Bureau of Labor Statistics is a great resource for information about careers. Let's say you want to search for occupations that pay well and don't require a college degree. Go to the Online Occupational Handbook at bls.gov/ooh/. At the top of the page is a pulldown menu allowing you to select occupations by pay, education, and other factors. As of the current edition of this book, transportation, storage, and distribution managers typically earn over $80,000 annually and don't require a college degree.

SEARCH BY GEOGRAPHY

Once you have a job title you're interested in and you want to know whether there are any openings in a specific part of the United States, visit careeronestop.org/Toolkit/Careers/Occupations/occupation-profile.aspx. On this site you can search by job title and location (zip code or state).

For example, a search for logistics managers in the LA Metro area shows that the occupation is expected to grow much faster than average, a bachelor's degree is generally required, and the median salary is around $80,000. (Note that that's the median salary for all people in this occupation, not the starting salary.) The site lists activities, skills, and qualifications associated with the job, as well as related jobs and current job openings.

CONSIDER A JOB THAT REQUIRES SOME POST-SECONDARY EDUCATION

Some decent-paying jobs require training beyond high school, but not a four-year degree. U.S. News lists the 25 highest-paying jobs that don't require a college degree at money.usnews.com/money/careers/slideshow/25-best-jobs-that-dont-require-a-college-degree. These include insurance salesperson (median salary: $52,180), wind turbine technician (median salary: $56,230), and patrol officer (median salary: $65,540).

CONSIDER THE MILITARY

The U.S. military provides training, housing, and job placement benefits. Tuition Assistance is an educational benefit provided to active service members; each branch of the service has its own requirements. You can see each service's requirements and benefits at military.com/education/money-for-school. In addition to tuition assistance, the Harry W. Colmery Veterans Educational Assistance Act, known as the GI Bill or the Forever GI Bill, provides educational benefits to those with 3 or more years of service. GI Bill benefits can be used for apprenticeship, vocational, bachelor's, and graduate education, and in some cases can be transferred to your spouse or children. Find out more about the GI Bill at benefits.va.gov/gibill/.

A military career is not for everyone. Success in the military requires physical and mental endurance, and a willingness to follow orders. When you enlist, don't just sign on the dotted line. Negotiate, read your enlistment contract carefully, and don't believe any promises that aren't written in the contract. Read more before you make any life-changing decisions:

liveabout.com/what-the-recruiter-never-told-you-3332714

military.com/join-armed-forces.

MORE EDUCATED PEOPLE THAN JOBS

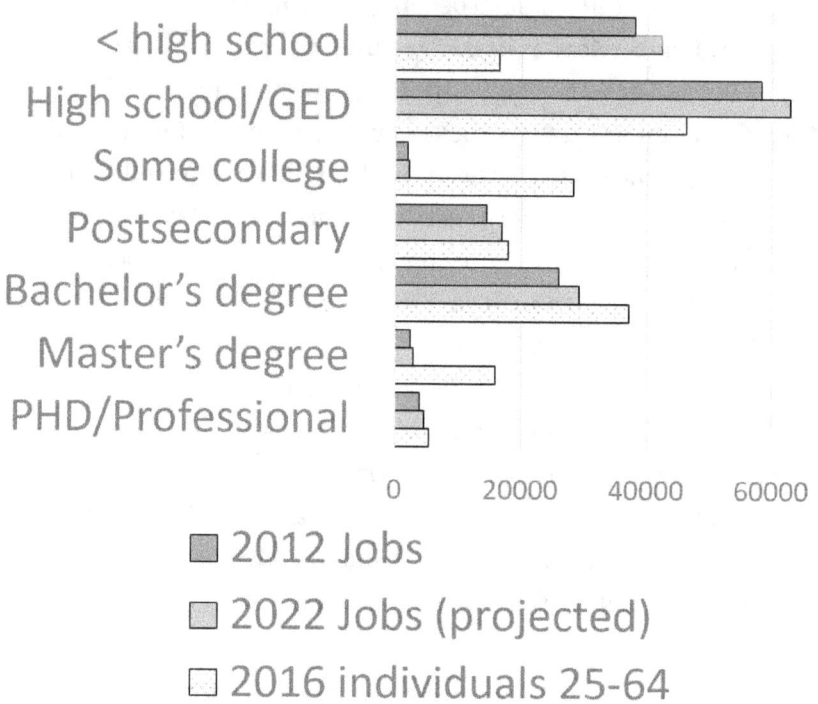

There are more college-educated people than jobs requiring a college education

5

SO YOU'RE GOING TO COLLEGE

If you are planning to attend college and you are in high school right now, **enroll in college prep or Advanced Placement courses and take as much math and writing as you can**. This will keep your options open, no matter what you decide later. And start saving. Everyone talks about tuition costs, but books and living expenses can add up too. The following checklist starts in the first year of high school, but **if you didn't start planning for college at age 14, don't worry**. Read over the suggestions and **use whatever makes sense for you**.

FRESHMAN YEAR (first year of high school)

- Ask your guidance counselor or teachers what Advanced Placement courses are available, whether you are eligible, and how to enroll in them.
- Start your resume. Use it to keep a list of your awards, honors, paid and volunteer work, and extracurricular activities.
- Update your resume throughout high school. When you need to apply for jobs and scholarships, you don't need to hunt around for your information. You already have it in one file.

SOPHOMORE YEAR (second year of high school)

- Meet with your school counselor or mentor to discuss colleges and their requirements.
- The two main qualifying tests for getting into college are the SAT and the ACT. Practice for the SAT by taking a practice Preliminary SAT/National Merit Scholarship Qualifying Test (PSAT/NMSQT) at collegereadiness.collegeboard.org/psat-nmsqt-psat-10. If you don't have internet access or a printer, try the public library. Tell the librarian that you want to take a practice test. Many four-year institutions have made standardized tests optional. It's still a good idea to take them if you can. If your results aren't good, don't submit them. If you score in the top half of test-takers, your test results might tip the balance in your favor.
- For ACT practice, the Prepscholar site has a list of interactive and printable practice tests: blog.prepscholar.com/complete-official-act-practice-tests-free-links
- Make the best use of your summers: Work, volunteer, or take a summer course. You can enroll in noncredit courses, and sometimes even credit courses, at a nearby community college or four-year institution.
- Plan to attend career and college fairs to talk to recruiters and get a more in-depth look at your options.
- Research majors that might be a good fit with your interests and goals based on your results from the U.S. Department of Labor's career search at bls.gov/careeroutlook/. But bear in mind that most high school students have no idea what careers are out there, much less which career is best suited for them. Even those rare students who do decide on a career track early in life may find themselves changing careers every few years once they're in the workplace.
- Keep taking **math classes** and try to sequence your classes to complete calculus while you're in high school. Successful completion of calculus is associated with success in college in general, and in science and technology specifically [87, 88]. Not completing calculus in high school closes off your options. If your high school doesn't offer calculus, consider taking it

at a community college over the summer.

JUNIOR YEAR (third year of high school)

- If you are planning to enter a four-year school right out of high school: Take the PSAT/NMSQT in the fall. You must take the test in 11th grade to qualify for scholarships and programs associated with the National Merit Scholarship Program. Check with your high school for the schedule.
- If you are planning to enter a four-year school right out of high school: Register for and take the SAT and ACT for college admission. Your high school counselor should be able to tell you when and how to register. If your family is low income, or if you are an orphan, in foster care, or a ward of the state, you may qualify for a waiver. If you plan to start out at a community college, you won't need SAT or ACT scores. If your high school will subsidize the cost, it might be worth taking the test. A good test score can tip the scales if you decide to apply to a selective institution later on.
- It's not too early to start looking for scholarship money! Use the Department of Labor's scholarship search at careeronestop.org/toolkit/training/find-scholarships.aspx. Some deadlines fall as early as the summer between 11th and 12th grades, so prepare now to submit applications soon.

SUMMER BETWEEN JUNIOR AND SENIOR YEAR: THE INFAMOUS FAFSA

You must fill out the FAFSA, or Free Application for Federal Student Aid, even if you don't think you qualify for federal student aid. Having filled it out is a prerequisite for scholarships, even those not based on financial need. Fill it out at fafsa.ed.gov. Note the .gov suffix, meaning that the site is run by the Federal government. **Do not fill out the FAFSA at a non-.gov site, and do not pay to fill it out.**

On the FAFSA site you will create a username and password called the FSA ID. You'll use your FSA ID to confirm your identity when accessing your financial aid information later. You must create your own FSA ID. If your parent creates it for you, that will cause confusion later and will slow down the financial aid application process.

For more information, go to the Federal Student Aid Information Center at studentaid.gov/help-center/contact

SENIOR YEAR (fourth year of high school)

Early Decision and Early Action

Some institutions offer Early Action or Early Decision. Both are ways for students and institutions to "lock in" decisions. Early **decision** plans are binding, meaning if you apply and are accepted, you must attend the college. You may only apply to one college using Early Decision. Early decision plans do not allow applicants to shop around for the best financial aid package.

Early **action** plans are a little more flexible. Students apply early and receive an early response but are under no obligation to accept an offer. You can learn more about Early Decision and Early Action at professionals.college-board.org/guidance/applications/early .

Financial Aid: Grants, work-study, or loans?

Federal student aid comes in three flavors: Grants, work-study, and loans.

Grants are free money. Take them whenever they're offered.

Work-study is a program under which the Federal government subsidizes your employment on campus. This is a pretty good deal, as students with on-campus jobs usually have an easier time coordinating their work and school schedules and do better in school as a result.

In addition, depending on what your responsibilities are, you might have an opportunity to get to know your professors and/or staff members better and to make a positive impression on them. This can come in handy for building your network. You can draw on your contacts if you need career help or letters of recommendation later.

Student loans should be approached with caution. Defaulting on a loan can have catastrophic consequences. Default rates are higher for those who do not finish their degrees or who attend for-profit institutions [104]. Unlike other loans, student loans are nearly impossible to discharge in bankruptcy [105]. While you may read about students graduating with hundreds of thousands of dollars in student loan debt, this is unusual. Most students who default have a relatively small balance. It's not necessarily bad to have a moderate amount of loan debt that you can afford to repay. What you want to avoid is defaulting on your loan.

If you do take out a loan, plan to start paying off your loan the minute you graduate. Even a single missed deadline can get you into trouble. You can read more about types of student aid at studentaid.gov/understand-aid/types

The Western Undergraduate Exchange

The Western Undergraduate Exchange is an agreement among the states belonging to the Western Interstate Commission for Higher Education (WICHE). If you are a resident of one of these states, the Western Undergraduate Exchange program gives you discounted tuition in participating schools in any of these states: Alaska, Arizona, California, Colorado, Guam, Hawai'i, Idaho, Montana, Nevada, New Mexico, North Dakota, Northern Mariana Islands, Oregon, South Dakota, Utah, Washington, and Wyoming. See wiche.edu/wue for details.

The SAT and the ACT

The SAT and the ACT are two standardized tests commonly used in college admissions. Schools will generally accept either one. If you don't test well or wish to avoid standardized tests for other reasons, consider a "test optional" school. There are currently over 1800. You can find a list of them at fairtest.org/university/optional.

You may also wish to take the test and decide later whether to submit the results. Some high schools offer free or subsidized ACT and/or SAT testing. Ask your high school counselor about this.

Another way to take standardized tests for free is if you are from a low-income household. Instructions for **SAT** fee waivers are at collegereadiness.collegeboard.org/sat/register/fees/fee-waivers . Instructions for ACT fee waivers are at act.org/content/act/en/products-and-services/the-act/registration/fees.html#feewaivers

College Applications

It can cost $100 or more to apply to a single institution; applying to several can add up. Ask your counselor whether your high school provides financial aid for application fees. If not, many universities will waive application fees for financial need or good academic performance. You need to inquire with the schools individually to see what their policy is. Be persistent; sometimes four-year schools will have special events or promotions.

The Common Application

The Common Application is a single application that lets you apply to over 1,000 institutions using one form. It can save you a lot of time and effort, and it's free for the applicant, although individual schools may still require their own application fee. You can find it at commonapp.org.

To apply, you'll need:

- A copy of your high school transcript
- A list of extracurricular activities, both school-related and non-school-related
- Test scores and dates from your college entrance exams (SATs, ACTs, SAT Subject Tests)
- PARENT / LEGAL GUARDIAN INFORMATION including educational background, occupational information, employer information, etc.

The Coalition for College has 114 member schools using their application and is available at coalitionforcollegeaccess.org.

Don't be afraid to apply to schools you think you can't afford. If you have documentable financial need, you may be able to get your application fee waived. Wealthy schools with large endowments can afford generous financial aid and may be more affordable than your state school. Examine aid offers carefully and look for grants or scholarships, not loans.

Schools that meet your financial need without loans

Certain highly competitive schools will meet your entire financial need, without loans. The trick is to get accepted in the first place. The schools are Amherst College (MA), Bowdoin College (ME), Brown University (RI), Columbia University (NY), Davidson College (NC), Harvard University (MA), Massachusetts Institute of Technology, Pomona College (CA), Princeton University (NJ), Stanford University (CA), Swarthmore College (PA), University of Michigan—Ann Arbor, University of North Carolina—Chapel Hill, Washington and Lee University (VA), Amherst College (MA), Bowdoin College (ME), Brown University (RI), and Columbia University (NY).

See usnews.com/education/best-colleges/paying-for-college/articles/schools-that-meet-full-financial-need-with-no-loans for the latest updates.

Spring Semester of your senior year

- Visit colleges that have invited you to enroll, if you can afford the travel.
- Review your college acceptances and compare the colleges' financial aid offers.
- Contact a school's financial aid office if you have questions about the aid that school has offered you. In fact, getting to know your financial aid staff early is a good idea no matter what—they can tell you about deadlines, other aid for which you might wish to apply, and important paperwork you might need to submit.
- When you decide which school you want to attend, notify that school of your commitment, and submit any required financial deposit. Many schools require this notification and deposit by May 1.

Does school prestige matter?

Do you need to go to a "top" school? It depends. If your goal is to work for an elite investment bank or to clerk for a Supreme Court justice, then you should shoot for Harvard or Yale [81, 106]. Otherwise, your alma mater is less important than your personal qualities and your major. Full-time employed women with a BA degree from the most selective schools earn about as much as men who graduate from the least selective schools. Business and health majors from the least selective schools earn about as much as education majors from the most selective schools [107]. Institution attended explains only a small amount of the variation in college graduates' earnings [108].

Life satisfaction after graduation is associated with the following experiences, no matter what kind of college you attended [109]:

- Engaging in meaningful jobs or internships
- Choosing courses requiring long-term work.
- Getting all the financial aid possible and available
- Working an on-campus job
- Keeping paid employment to under 20 hours a week.
- Keeping debt under $25K

IF YOU'VE BEEN OUT OF SCHOOL FOR A WHILE

The advice above may not apply if you left high school a few years ago.

- Consider a General Educational Development (GED) certificate if you don't have a high school diploma. Search online for "GED certificate" and your state's name.
- Research career possibilities using the Occupational Outlook Handbook at bls.gov/ooh and the career search tools at mynextmove.org and careeronestop.org. Your local community college will have career counselors willing to work with you.
- Consider starting at a community college and use College Navigator at

nces.ed.gov/collegenavigator to find the right four-year school to transfer to.
- Ask employers to recommend schools that provide training in the skills you will need for the career you choose.
- Ask your employer if assistance is available to help you pay for school.
- Use the U.S. Department of Labor's scholarship search at careeronestop.org/toolkit/training/find-scholarships.aspx to find scholarships.
- Apply for federal student aid by filling out the Free Application for Federal Student Aid: studentaid.ed.gov/sa/fafsa/filling-out.
- Get to know the financial aid staff at the school you plan to attend; they can help you with aid applications and explain the types of aid available.

CHOOSING A MAJOR

Your own human capital—skills, work habits, ability to read others' emotions and control your own—will make a huge impact on your life and career. But when it comes to starting salary, major matters. Engineering, computer science, and finance majors make a lot of money; art, education and social work majors don't. You can see earnings by major from the National Center for Education Statistics at nces.ed.gov/programs/coe/indicator_sbc.asp. If you want to make a good salary right out of college, pick something with "Engineering" in the title. But you may have concerns other than salary. You might value security of employment or having a job that fits your interests. For example, early childhood education majors don't earn much, but they also have a low unemployment rate. You can find unemployment and underemployment by major at newyorkfed.org/research/college-labor-market/index.html#/outcomes-by-major

NO, YOU CAN'T BE AN ASTRONAUT

Will this be you? Probably not.

6

ONCE YOU'RE IN, MAKE THE MOST OF IT

The transition from high school to college can be jarring, especially for students who didn't have to work that hard in high school. Suddenly most of your day is unstructured, and it seems you can spend most of your day goofing off without any negative consequences. You can't.

LEARN TO USE YOUR STUDY TIME

Watch Stephen Chew's video series, How to Get the Most out of Studying: youtube.com/playlist?list=PL85708E6EA236E3DB. The videos are between five and ten minutes each, and well worth your time. Among other things, you will find that you're not necessarily the best judge of how much you're learning, that popular study methods like highlighting the textbook are not that effective, and that good old flashcards work really well.

ALWAYS SHOW UP FOR CLASS, EVEN IF IT'S NOT "REQUIRED"

Spending time in the classroom will not only help you to learn the material but can help you to make a good impression on the professor. Why would you care about that? Because you're not just after a passing grade. You need to start building relationships now that you can draw on later for job referrals and letters of recommendation.

DEVOTE AT LEAST TWO HOURS OUT OF CLASS STUDYING FOR EVERY HOUR YOU SPEND IN CLASS

This isn't some arbitrary rule professors made up to torture you. The credit hour is based on the Carnegie Unit, which arose in the late 19th century in order to standardize workload. One credit hour is equivalent to one hour of classroom or direct faculty instruction and a minimum of two hours of out of class student work each week for approximately fifteen weeks for one semester [110]. This is why 12 semester credits can be considered a full-time load. It's expected that in addition to the 12 hours you're spending in class, you're spending an additional 24 to 36 hours outside of class, studying and doing homework.

STAY INFORMED

Keep on top of relevant news in your industry and take every opportunity to enhance your general knowledge. Being well-informed will help you in the classroom and in the workplace, and will make your world a more interesting place to live in. Podcasts are a timesaver. You can listen while you are driving or doing chores. Choose general-interest podcasts about current events, economics, history, and science.

GET AN INTERNSHIP BEFORE YOUR SENIOR YEAR

Your part-time retail or work-study job is certainly work, and it might have aspects that look good on a resume. But the kind of job you are likely to have in college won't give you professional experience. This is where internships come in. (Internship-like experiences might also be called externships or co-ops.) Go to your school's internship or career office if you have one. If your school does not have a career or internship office, talk to your professors to let them know you are interested in internships. You may be able to set up an internship as a directed study.

CREATE A LINKEDIN ACCOUNT

If you don't have one already, create a LinkedIn account. LinkedIn has become the social network of choice for professional networking. While you're still a student, it's appropriate to use your .edu email account. When you graduate and transition into the workforce, you will want to use an email account set aside for professional use.

Find keywords for your LinkedIn description.

Look for job and internship openings that interest you. Copy several of them and paste the text into a text file. Open a word cloud generator like tagcrowd.com or wordclouds.com. Paste in the text from the ads you've collected and generate your word cloud. See if you can work the most frequent or "big" words into your profile.

Take advantage of your profile options.

Fill out all the available sections including Courses, Projects, Languages, Certifications, and Organizations.

Connect

Use LinkedIn to connect with your professors, classmates, and acquaintances. Because LinkedIn is a professional network, not a social one, people at your school or workplace will tend to react positively to a connection request.

DON'T DO ANYTHING DUMB ON SOCIAL MEDIA

Other than LinkedIn, it's safest to avoid social media entirely, but that may not be realistic. In any case, don't post, email, or write anything you wouldn't want the world—and specifically, your employer—to see. People have lost their jobs over imprudent self-expression on social media [111]. Avoid politics (not all employers will share your views). Don't post pictures of yourself in costume. A topical costume may seem funny at the time but may not age well.

Don't post anything about drug use or drinking. Drinking alcohol is perfectly legal if you are of age, but that didn't stop a teacher from losing her job over a private Facebook photo showing her drinking while she was on vacation [112].

School can be frustrating, but don't announce your intention to injure or murder your professor. This can get you a visit from the FBI [113]. (On the bright side, you won't have to worry about your job search or living expenses for a few years).

7

LOOK FOR A JOB

If you did an internship and it worked out well, you might have a job offer in hand before you graduate. Congratulations! And be careful. Some companies will withdraw your offer if they find out you're looking for another job. Find out if this is the case. If you're allowed to shop around, do. You'll be in a strong negotiating position as you already have an offer in hand.

If you don't have a job lined up by the start of your senior year, you might have trouble finding something. The summer before your final year of college is a great time to secure your first job.

YOUR SOCIAL NETWORK (THE REAL-LIFE KIND)

No later than the beginning of your senior year, go to the professors you really clicked with, and ask them whether they would be willing to be a reference for you. Do the same with staff members and anyone you worked for. At this point you don't need to ask them to write recommendation letters. Keep their names and email addresses on hand, ready to provide as references should anyone ask. When you ask for a letter, be prepared to take "no" for an answer. It's better to have someone honestly decline than to provide you a weak or negative reference.

As you revisit your social network, people may try to give you advice. Listen and thank them. Their intentions are probably good, and they most likely just want to help. If the advice turns out not to be useful, then don't use it. But make a note of it, and keep an open mind.

YOUR ELEVATOR PITCH

An elevator pitch is a thirty-second version of your story. The idea of the elevator pitch is that if you find yourself in an elevator with your ideal employer, you can introduce yourself and make a good impression in the short time you have together. Professional services firm PwC suggests composing your elevator pitch in three parts:

1. **Who are you?** "Hello, my name is Penny Priddy. I'm a senior at Fugue State University, majoring in aeronautical engineering with a minor in music history."
2. **What are your unique accomplishments, interests, and skills?** "I interned last summer at Yoyodyne Propulsion Systems, where I worked on the design of the YP-100 oscillation overthruster and developed a passion for interdimensional teambuilding."
3. **What do you want?** "I saw that your company is expanding its interdimensional research efforts, which is why I came this conference. I'm very interested in the mission of the Banzai Institute, and I would like to work for the Banzai Institute's Research and Development Division."

For more detail, see PwC's worksheet at pwc.com/c1/en/assets/downloads/personal_brand_workbook.pdf

YOUR ONLINE PRESENCE

Your future employers (as well as employees, coworkers, romantic prospects, and acquaintances) will search for you online. Because you paid attention to the previous chapter, your social media profile is blameless and squeaky-clean. Good job!

But just to be on the safe side, set up a Google alert on your name. That way, you'll see when something gets posted about you. If you have a very common name, you might want to add more detail to avoid getting inundated with irrelevant email alerts.

Go to Google Alerts at google.com/alerts. At the top of the page is a box with a magnifying glass icon. Enter your name and select the "Create Alert" button that appears. Then select how often you want to get alerts (once a week is probably enough) and other options. Once you set this up, you will get an email when your name is mentioned online.

YOUR EMAIL ADDRESS

Set up a separate, professional-sounding email address to use for job searches and professional activities. Do not use it for social, leisure, or family communication. You will use this professional email address to sign up for LinkedIn and other job-related services and to communicate with employers and recruiters.

A Gmail address is generally considered to be more work-appropriate than Yahoo, AOL, or Hotmail, which are best used for personal communication. Before you sign up, set up a free Gmail account that is exclusively for job-related things. Using the name Patience Fairweather as an example, the format patience.fairweather [at] gmail.com or p.fairweather [at] gmail.com will work.

Mail.com offers free email accounts with a selection of domains. If one of the available domains suits your career aspirations, you may want to get an address like p.fairweather@consultant.com or patience@therapist.net.

If you want your email address customized, as in patience@fairweather.com, you'll need a custom domain. For this you will need to purchase a domain name at a site like namecheap.com and follow the instructions there to set up your email account.

FUN SOCIAL MEDIA: FACEBOOK, TWITTER, INSTAGRAM, SNAPCHAT, ETC.

If you have social media accounts, make sure to keep your personal and professional separate, and to have strong privacy settings on your personal accounts. Detailed instructions for adjusting Facebook privacy settings are at facebook.com/help/325807937506242. Facebook knows a lot about you, including things you never meant to tell it [114].

If you leave town for an interview or any other reason, don't post anything about travel plans until after you return from your trip. You don't want to lay out the welcome mat for burglars, and you don't want potential employers to think you're naïve about security.

SERIOUS SOCIAL MEDIA: LINKEDIN

If you're looking for a job, you need a LinkedIn profile. It may be the first thing that comes up when someone searches for you online, so it must look good. A strong profile can help you build your resume, keep connected with your alumni network, and maintain an online presence that will enhance your job search.

If you don't already have a LinkedIn profile, it's straightforward to set one up. Go to linkedin.com. If you're not logged in, you'll be invited to join the site.

Setting up your account will take some time and thought. You'll be asked to enter information about your education, work experience, publications, and skills.

BUILDING YOUR RESUME

Once you've completed your LinkedIn page, you'll have a head start on your resume. Some companies will let you apply to jobs using your LinkedIn account as your resume. This can save you a lot of time, but those employers are the exception.

Most employers still require a separate application and a resume tailored to the specific position. Still, having a standard resume to work from can be a big help.

It's not necessary to bother with fancy formatting, as most resumes are now machine scanned by an Applicant Tracking System (ATS). Your application has a better chance if your resume is easy to scan. To compose a machine-readable resume, follow this outline:

MACHINE-READABLE RESUME OUTLINE:

FIRSTNAME LASTNAME
    Mailing Address
    Phone number you can answer anytime
    A professional email address
    OBJECTIVE or SUMMARY
    You can pull from a summary from your elevator pitch
    KEYWORDS
    Optional; for important keywords that don't seem to fit anywhere else
    EDUCATION
    Most recent first
    If you are a new graduate, put any honors like the Dean's List here
    EXPERIENCE
    Put job-relevant experience here. For each position, list an accomplishment. For example, increased daily page visits from 10 to 100
    OTHER EXPERIENCE
    Optional. Semesters abroad, unrelated internships and honors
    ACTIVITIES
    Optional. Clubs, sports, volunteer work
    SKILLS and CERTIFICATIONS
    This section is very important. Put certifications and specific software skills here

TIPS FOR MACHINE-READABLE RESUMES:

- Executive resume writer Lisa Rangel suggests **putting your name and the desired position as the title**: "Your Name – Marketing Director."
- **Be specific** when describing your past positions and accomplishments. Use employer names; omitting them can seem like you're hiding something. Include any achievement that can be described in numbers like "Increased revenues by 30%."
- Adecco's Jenni Chelenyak recommends using a separate line for each element of your contact information and ending company names with terms like LLC, Inc., Co., and Corp. **This helps the software recognize the companies** and put them in the right category.
- Use **Arial, Helvetica, or Times Roman in 10 or 12-point font**. These are considered standard and most scanners will be able to handle them.
- Use **recognizable words** in the headings: Objective / Summary, Experience, Employment, Work History, Positions Held, Appointments, Skills, Summary, Summary of Qualifications, Accomplishments, Strengths, Education, Affiliations, Professional Affiliations, Publications, Papers, Licenses, Certifications, Examinations, Honors, Personal.
- **Do not combine two headings into one**. Avoid rare or unusual words.
- An **Objectives** section is appropriate for a new job seeker; a **Career Summary** is appropriate for someone with substantial work experience.
- Use **Rich Text Format (RTF)** for your resume unless the application instructions tell you otherwise. Test your resume's readability by copying and pasting it into a **simple text editor** like WordPad.
- Don't use underlining or other formatting.
- Scan your resume to see what the machine sees at **jobscan.co**.
- If you don't mind signing up for a mailing list, submit your resume to **topresume.com/resume-review** for a free critique.
- For more on crafting your resume, go to Purdue's Online Writing Lab: **owl.purdue.edu**

People are still part of the process. If you have a friend or relative who works in Human Resources, manages employees, or reads a lot of resumes, have them look over yours. Or go to your college's career center for help. You don't have to take every suggestion they give you but listen to their feedback. You are likely to learn something useful.

NO, YOU CAN'T BE AN ASTRONAUT

"Shoot for the moon. Even if you miss, you'll land among the stars."

"Have the courage to follow your heart."

"Stop looking forward to Fridays and start looking forward to Mondays!"

"Do what you love and you'll never work a day in your life!"

Do not believe any of this for a second

8

THE JOB SEARCH

Whether you're still in school or switching jobs or careers, be prepared to spend a lot of time and effort on finding a job. **Treat your job search like a job in itself**—a job with no boss to guide you, no co-workers to commiserate with, and no HR department to complain to. You'll need to be persistent, organized, and thick-skinned.

KEEP TRACK OF YOUR APPLICATIONS

Technology has made it easy to apply for jobs. Instead of printing out resumes and cover letters on fancy paper and paying for postage, you can apply for jobs entirely online. But this means that the companies you want to work for are likely getting hundreds of applications for each open position.

In addition, many posted jobs don't really exist. Some job "interviews" are really an attempt to get industry or competitor information; some jobs are not quite as advertised, for example commission-only instead of salaried; some positions are going to an inside applicant, but the rules require a national search. This means you should plan on sending out hundreds of applications. An app called JibberJobber (JibberJobber.com) can help you keep track of your search. It's free for up to 25 contacts, so you can use it and decide whether you like it before paying for a subscription.

You can also create your own job search spreadsheet. Templates can be found at templates.office.com/en-us/Job-application-log-TM16400610 and docs.google.com/spreadsheets/d/1b4_lpHeLb9NldVWgWKq14nMxHEvlF3qMpEd3QdOc7Ck/edit#gid=815296917 .

Every time you send out an application or get a response, make the appropriate entry in the spreadsheet. Make sure your spreadsheet is somewhere you can access. Use a service like Dropbox or Google Drive and back it up regularly. If you happen to be away from your desk when you get a call, you'll want to the information available to you.

SET UP DAILY EMAIL ALERTS

If your college or university has an active career office, sign up for any services they offer. Whether you are working with a career services office or not, make sure you have job announcements coming into your mailbox every day. Here are instructions on how to set up job alerts:

LinkedIn

SETTING UP A JOB ALERT ON LINKEDIN:

- Click the briefcase icon at the top of the page to search for a job on LinkedIn. On the upper left-hand corner of the page, you will see the search window.
- At the top of the left panel of the job search results page, switch the Job alert toggle to On to create a job alert for your current search criteria.
- Or set-up a job alert by switching the Create alert for this search toggle button at the bottom left of the search results page to On.
- In the Create search alert pop-up, select how often you'd like to receive alerts about new jobs on LinkedIn.com that fit those specific search parameters from the Receive alert dropdown. The available options are daily or weekly.
- Select how you'd like to get notified from the Get notified via dropdown. The available options are email, notifications, and email & notifications.
- Click Save.

USAJobs (U.S. citizens and legal residents)

SETTING UP A JOB ALERT ON USAJOBS

- Sign into USAJOBS. If you don't have a profile, you need to create one. Only signed in users can save their search.
- Start a job search by entering a keyword or location in the search box and click Search.
- Narrow your results using filters.
- Click Save this search on the search results page located above the search results.
- Name your search—this will help you manage your saved searches.
- Choose how often you want to get notified. We recommend daily if you're looking for very specific jobs, since some jobs can open and close within a week.
- Click Save.

Other job search sites to investigate:

- CareerBuilder.com
- RobertHalf.com
- Indeed.com
- Glassdoor.com
- Ziprecruiter.com/search-jobs
- Monster.com

Specialized Sites

- Accounting and finance: mycareer.aicpa-cima.com/
- Healthcare: healthcarejobsite.com, healthcareadministrationjobs.net
- Higher education: higheredjobs.com, insidehighered.com, chronicle.com.
- Programming and tech: Dice.com, TechCareers.com, Crunchboard.com.

YOUR DAILY SCHEDULE

If you are currently between jobs, you should plan to follow this schedule just as you would a regular job. It may help to take your laptop to a library or coffee shop, just to get out of the house and feel like you're at work.

If you are still in school, or currently employed, you'll only be able to use this schedule on weekends and holidays and will have to do what you can in your free hours during the week.

When is your brain at its best?

You need to figure out what time of day you are most productive. Once you know your best brain time, set aside those two hours or so for writing cover letters and customizing your resume. Use the less-productive hours for more routine tasks like sending out completed applications, filling in your tracking information, and finding new jobs to apply for.

Many people find they can concentrate for 20 minutes at a time, after which they start to lose focus. This varies among individuals, of course, but it's a general enough rule that there is a popular time-management method, called the Pomodoro Method, that involves working in 20-minute bursts with 5-minute breaks in between. (The method's inventor originally used an Italian kitchen timer shaped like a tomato—pomodoro is Italian for tomato—to time his work.) You can use this method to work through your most productive two hours.

How do you know when your brain is at its best? Observe yourself for a few days and see when you are most able to tackle challenging tasks like writing or starting a project. For more specific feedback on this, take the online questionnaire at chronotype-self-test.info/index.php?sid=61524&newtest=Y

SAMPLE WEEKDAY SCHEDULE for SOMEONE WHOSE PEAK TIME is 10 to NOON

7am:

Wake up, have a cup of coffee, take a half-hour walk, and come back and shower. This will start you off with mild exercise and sunlight, good for your cognition and mental health.

8-10am:

Because your brain's not fully up and running, do moderately-taxing tasks. Open your job search email account and go through the day's jobs. Save the ones you intend to apply for and record them on your spreadsheet. Delete the ones you do not intend to apply for.

Fix yourself breakfast.

Read some industry news.

Set up for your productive time:

Find the announcements for the jobs you are going to apply to, and similar jobs that may not be in your desired location.

Copy similar jobs into a single document.

Then copy and paste the text into a word cloud generator such as tagcrowd.com or wordclouds.com. In this word cloud for hotel manager positions, unexpected words include "experience," "vision," "financial," and "team." You now have general keywords for your cover letter. You might emphasize that you are fluent in the financial as well as the people aspects of the job, and that you can direct your team to translate your employer's vision into a consistent guest experience.

10am-noon:

This is your productive time. You will customize your resume and write a cover letter for each position.

Customizing your resume and cover letter

- Open up the word cloud generator again.

- Copy and paste in the text from the particular job you're applying to.
- Open a new window. Go to the company website and find the Mission Statement, the Vision Statement, and/or the "About Us" description. Paste these into the same word cloud box.
- Generate your company-specific word cloud.
- These keywords reflect the company's aspirations for itself. Work them in wherever they fit. You can even put them into the "keywords" section of your resume if appropriate.
- Some applications require a cover letter, while others make it optional. Always submit a cover letter if you can.
- In your cover letter, strike a tone that is confident but not overconfident. Flatter the employer ("It is with great pleasure that I am seeking an employment opportunity with your institution. It is a well-respected company and I would be proud to be a part of it.") [101]
- Before you submit your resume and cover letter, run a spell check. Then run the documents through a machine scan simulator like jobscan.co. What comes out of the machine scan should look like what's described in the job announcement.
- If the scan results don't look right, edit your resume and try again.
- Proofread everything before sending. A single typo can disqualify you.
- Focus on sending a few well-crafted applications to jobs that are a good match. Don't just blast out a generic resume to any position that's remotely a fit.
- As soon as you complete each application, record the relevant information into JibberJobber.com or your spreadsheet.

12pm-2pm:

Break for lunch. Turn off the computer. Go for a walk. Exercise. Do your grocery shopping. Get the laundry done. If you haven't showered or brushed your teeth yet, do it now.

2pm until bedtime:

Allocate your time among people-oriented activities like volunteering and networking, and solitary ones like reading industry news and relevant blogs. Alison Green, the woman behind the wonderful Ask a Manager blog (bookmark it now at askamanager.org) recommends boosting your job search by volunteering, reconnecting, and networking:

VOLUNTEERING

If you are currently not employed, consider volunteering. Volunteering has three advantages:

First, volunteering **helps other people**.

Second, volunteering can help you to **build your network** and get connected to job opportunities.

Finally, volunteering can help you to **avoid an obvious time gap in your resume** if you are between jobs. A mainstream organization such as the Red Cross or United Way will be appealing to most employers. A church-related organization might not carry as much weight with employers, as they may assume your service is simply part of your church membership. If you can get onto the board of a non-profit, that's ideal, but director positions are competitive. Any computer, bookkeeping, or marketing skills that you can contribute are likely to be useful and in high demand.

RECONNECTING

Invite your former co-workers, old bosses, and friends to lunch or coffee. Don't pressure them to provide you with job leads. Instead, use the time to catch up.

Reconnecting expands your network and the possibility of hearing about a position. It's also good for your mental health, as it helps you to avoid becoming too isolated.

If you are an introvert, try to force yourself to do this at least once a month.

Networking.

Join professional organizations in your field. Your local Chamber of Commerce or Junior Chamber of Commerce are a good start. Service clubs like Rotary, Kiwanis, or Lion's Club are a great way to meet local employers and benefit your community. Industry-specific associations can be helpful both for making contacts and keeping your knowledge current.

You might have the opportunity to take on a leadership position in one of these groups. If you can commit to doing the work well, do it. This will look great on your resume and will help you to build your network and generate goodwill.

YOUR PRE-INTERVIEW CHECKLIST

Congratulations, you've been invited to interview! Whether it's on the phone, via video, or in person, you need to prepare thoroughly beforehand.

Don't be like the young lady who, when interviewing with IBM, volunteered that she admired their "Xerox machines." Or the gentleman who, when asked why he had chosen to interview with a specific company during on-campus interviews, replied, "Because you guys were on the list." Neither one got the job.

Research the company:

- Find the company's mission statement and vision statement. Strictly speaking, the vision is where the company wants to be in the future ("A Yoyodyne personal interdimensional overthruster in every American household") while the mission is what the company does every day ("Yoyodyne is a vertically-integrated company that bakes quality into every part of the manufacturing process"). Some companies have only a mission statement or a vision statement, while others have both. Some have neither and opt instead for "about" or "who we are." Whatever the company calls it, get familiar with its stated purpose. You should be able to show your interviewer that you are familiar with the company's self-image and aspirations.

- Research the company's financial health, including any big decisions or events that might affect its future. Is the company publicly traded? That is, do they sell stocks on a stock exchange like NASDAQ? If so, they'll have an Investor Information page. That will provide information about the financial health of the company. Bloomberg.com, Yahoo Finance, and other free sites can also be a good source of company information.
- Whether the company is publicly traded or not, do an online search for news of the company. If the company is small, you might find something in the online archives of the local newspaper.
- See where the company operates. Are they local, nationwide, or international? Do they have international customers or partners, and if so, are you willing to travel internationally? If you don't have a current passport, be prepared to tell the interviewer that you are in the process of getting one. If you are a U.S. citizen, apply for a U.S. passport at usa.gov/passport.
- Find out where the department fits within the company. How does it work with or overlap other departments, and are there possible interdepartmental rivalries?
- Figure out the company's business model, or how it makes its money. For example, social media companies and search engines get their revenue not from the people who use their services, but from advertisers who want to reach those people. Printer companies don't make their money from selling printers; in fact, they often lose money on the printer itself but make it up by selling expensive printer cartridges.

Check LinkedIn

- Find out whether anyone you know works at that company or has a connection there. If you are comfortable contacting this person, reach out, share your good news (you are very excited about your upcoming interview with Yoyodyne's new Consumer Devices Division) and ask for any advice or tips your contact might have. People are generally happy to

be asked for advice.
- If you know the name of the person who will be interviewing you, you might want to look them up. But be aware that LinkedIn can tell them that you viewed their profile.

Find out about salaries and interview experiences at Glassdoor. You may be required to register to get access.

- Read the company's reviews at glassdoor.com/Reviews/index.htm, but keep an open mind. Anyone can post there.
- Look at the salary information, but again, keep in mind that it may not be entirely accurate: glassdoor.com/Salaries/index.htm

Prepare yourself

If you have an in-person interview:

- Make sure you know how to get there. Take a drive out to the interview location once or twice before your scheduled interview. Note how long it takes and what the parking situation is.
- Make copies of your resume and other important documents (cover letter, list of references, etc.) in advance. Don't expect that your interviewers will have read or remembered your resume.
- If you have multiple interviews scheduled, one or more may be via video call even though you are on site. Find out in advance if any of your interviews will be on video and if so, whether you need to bring your own laptop.

If you have a video interview:

- Have a paper copy of your resume close by or up on the screen. You don't want to blank if you're asked about specific details or dates.
- Test your setup beforehand and make sure the background is clean and

professional. A blank wall or a bookshelf (stocked with non-controversial books) will work. Video backgrounds can work well, but can eat up bandwidth and make bits of you head disappear when you move. A window looking out on a view may be nice, but beware of being upstaged by weather, wildlife, or passers-by.

Whether your interview is in person or over video:

- Do your best to memorize your elevator pitch (have a printout handy as well). This is what you'll use to answer the "tell me about yourself" question.
- Prepare to be asked, "Why are you leaving your current job?" This doesn't apply if you're interviewing straight out of school, but if you are leaving another job, the right answer is something like "I'm happy where I am, but I'm looking for the opportunity to develop XYZ skill and/or work with XYZ technology." Never, never badmouth your employer or co-workers.
- Prepare to answer the question, "Why do you want to work for us?" This is the corporate equivalent of "tell me you love me." Pick something the company is likely to be proud of. "Yoyodyne products are the best in the industry and I'd be honored to work with the world-class engineers in the Consumer Devices Division."
- If you can do this discreetly, take down the names of everyone you meet, whether in individual or group settings, so that you can send appropriate thank-you notes later. For example, your interview schedule may indicate that you are meeting with the "quality control department" but if eight people show up and the company website shows eleven members of the department, you won't know whom to thank for meeting with you in person.
- Prepare an answer to the question, "What's your greatest weakness?"

What's your greatest weakness?

To respond to this question, pick something that is true, fixable, and not a dealbreaker for your potential employer. Your weakness might be something like,

"I'm an introvert, so in my previous sales job that involved ten straight hours of cold-calling, I found that I was getting a little worn-out toward the end of the day."

Then talk about how you're working on it: "I've been very deliberate about getting sufficient sleep, exercising regularly, and packing an energy bar when I have a day of dealing with people ahead of me. I've found that this way I can put in twelve-hour workdays with no drop in energy, and last month I was the most productive salesperson on my team."

Your answers should take the company culture into account. Some interviewers want to hear "I make sure to take care of myself and get enough sleep, because work-life balance is important" while others prefer "I'm training myself to be increasingly productive at work."

Prepare to be asked whether you have any questions of your own.

The worst response is probably something like, "so you guys don't do background checks or anything, right?" But the second-worst response is, "no, I don't have any questions." Consultant Rachel Weingarten recommends asking your interviewer questions like these:

- Why did you join the company? Does the interviewer seem genuinely happy about the job and the company? If they can't think of anything nice to say, that may be a red flag.
- How does this role further your company's mission? This will give you an idea of where the job you're interviewing for fits into the big picture, and whether its occupant is likely to have built-in enemies.
- Tell me about your most successful employees. What do they do differently? The answer will tell you a lot about what the company values.

- What do you expect someone in this position to accomplish in the first 60-90 days? It's good to know what their expectations are.
- What, if anything, in my background gives you pause? The answer may give you a chance to address concerns, in the interview and/or in your thank-you note.
- What is the turnover in the department I'm interviewing for? This is a tricky one; if you sense this question may make them defensive, don't ask it. But higher than average turnover for the industry might be a red flag.
- What are the opportunities for growth and advancement? This is good to know and assures your interviewer that you're looking at staying for the long term.
- If you had a chance to interview for your company again, knowing what you know now, what questions would you ask next time? The answer can be very informative. Your interviewer might even enjoy sharing some insight.
- What haven't I asked that most candidates ask? Your interviewer may not know how to answer this one. But if you do get an answer, it's likely to be a useful one.
- What are the next steps in this process? This is a graceful way to end your questions, and you want to know the answer anyway.

Once you have prepared answers and questions, conduct at least one practice interview, and ideally run through it two or three times. Your college career center might be able to set up a practice interview for you, but if not, a friend, family member, or roommate can do it. Don't skip this step. Tell your "interviewer" to be tough on you. Have them ask a few "illegal" questions about your age, family, marital status, or ethnic background. Practice now and you're less likely to choke when it happens for real.

The day before the interview

- Make sure you have stamps, nice notecards, and a decent pen. You will be writing a thank-you note, and a handwritten note is usually preferable. A set of simple, cream-colored thank-you cards, and a blue or black gel pen are good choices. Emailed acknowledgements are also acceptable, and have the advantage of getting to the recipient more quickly.
- Only when you've prepared all your answers and questions should you think about what to wear. Don't spend hours picking out your interview ensemble and procrastinating on everything else.
- You want your interviewers to remember you, not your outfit. Check the company's website to see how the managers dress. If you're not sure of the company's dress code, err on the side of caution. When in doubt, cover tattoos, knees, elbows, belly, shoulders, and cleavage. Jewelry shouldn't jangle. Shoes should cover the toes and be suitable for walking long distances. Make sure your clothing and shoes are comfortable.

The day of the interview

- You might be too nervous to eat breakfast. For an in-person interview pack a small bottle of water and a protein bar. It's okay to ask for a bathroom break between interview sessions if you need one. If you start to get lightheaded from hunger, use your bathroom break to wolf down your protein bar.
- If you're prone to headaches, take a non-prescription headache remedy like naproxen or ibuprofen before you go. Bring some with you as well.
- Make sure you're clean, showered, and deodorized, but don't wear fragrance. Some people are sensitive to strong scents. Leaving your interviewer gasping for air or breaking out in hives won't help your chances.
- Aim to arrive at the interview location 20 minutes early, and walk in 5-10 minutes early. For online interviews, log in five minutes early and test the video and microphone before the interview starts. Your interviewers

won't care that you got stuck behind the traffic accident of the century, or that your operating system started updating. If you're not there when they expect you, you've lost the job.
- When you first meet your interviewer smile and make direct eye contact. For video interviews, this means looking at the camera, not at the face on the screen. If in person, give a brief but firm handshake.
- Act like you are happy to be there and excited about meeting everyone and finding out more about the company.
- If you are physically entering an office, don't sit until your interviewer invites you to sit.
- Never interrupt your interviewer.
- Your interviewer is not supposed to ask about your age, marital status, sexual orientation, age, race, religion, nationality, or family. Nor should they ask what year you graduated from high school (a way of asking your age) or whether you have questions about the school district (a way of finding out whether you have children). Asking such questions opens the employer to charges of illegal discrimination. Some will ask these types of questions anyway, often innocently. It's up to you how to respond. You can answer the question; you can give the answer to the question you think they're really asking ("it sounds like you're looking for someone who can work after 5pm. I can work after-hours whenever needed."); or you can pretend to mishear and change the subject.
- Make sure to confirm each interviewer's name and if you are in person and it seems appropriate, ask for a business card. This will make you seem engaged and will help you to write your thank-you notes afterwards.

After the interview

As soon as you get home, record the details of your interview on your spreadsheet or on JibberJobber.com. Then send a thank-you note to everyone who interviewed you.

A SAMPLE THANK-YOU NOTE

Dear Dr. Lizardo [make sure to use the recipient's preferred title],

    Thank you for the opportunity to interview with Yoyodyne Propulsion Systems. Speaking with you last Wednesday has confirmed my desire to join the Yoyodyne team. I really appreciated learning more about the Pocket Overthruster project and am eager to be a part of your new Consumer Devices Division. Please do not hesitate to contact me if you have any further questions.

    Sincerely,
    Penny Priddy
    Penny.Priddy@gmail.com

9

MAKE YOURSELF FIRE-RESISTANT

Libraries have been written on how to be successful in the workplace, so we will just hit a few high points here.

WORK IS NOT SCHOOL

Although it may not have felt like it when you were a student, school is about meeting the student's needs. Work is about meeting the employer's needs. In the words of Suzanne Lucas, better known as Evil HR Lady,

> If you can't do the work, you're out. In school, they bring in specialists to help, and parents hover and work with you to bring grades up. Some bad parents (yes, I said it) simply demand that the school change a grade so that their little darling doesn't suffer any adverse consequences. In the workplace, we simply fire you. Sometimes we'll give you a 90-day performance improvement plan, but that's about it. [115]

CONFORM

Work is not the place to "be yourself." Nonconformity is generally frowned upon in any workplace. Offenses can include dressing too fashionably or not fashionably enough, having hobbies and interests that are too elitist, too low-class, or too weird, working too hard or not working hard enough, having different speech patterns, being in the minority regarding race, gender, age, ability, or body size, or being single when everyone else is married or vice versa.

Not all of these are under your control, and in a just world you wouldn't have to worry about them. But being different does make you stand out, and if you don't fit in, expect to be held to higher standards than others.

Consider the case of two co-workers who carpooled to work and walked through the door at the same time every morning. Sometimes they were on time, and other times they were one or two minutes late.

One day one of them was called into the boss's office. She was written up for lateness, put on a performance improvement plan, bumped to a lower pay band, and told she would have to punch a time clock that the boss had procured and placed on her desk. Her co-worker—who had been equally tardy—suffered no consequences. In fact, he was amazed and horrified for her.

The two employees worked in the same area and had similar job descriptions. But only the one who didn't look like most of her co-workers was singled out for discipline. Employees who don't fit in have less room for error. Is this fair? No. Does it really happen? All the time [116].

So what can you do? Fit in to the extent that you can, and don't give your detractors any ammunition.

MAKE A GOOD IMPRESSION

- Dress like everyone else (or at least don't look so different that you stand out).
- Keep quiet about any unconventional hobbies (some workplace cultures

frown on all hobbies, as they occupy time that might be spent working).
- Use the same vocabulary, and speak at the same level, as your boss. Err on the side of using simpler vocabulary.
- Come in early [117] and give the impression of putting in in a full day's work even if others don't.
- Never talk about how you work harder than everyone else.
- If you're invited to lunch, accept, but bring your own car so you won't be late getting back to the office.
- Participate in work-social activities, even if you would rather not.
- If you must leave your desk, leave a note ("in design meeting, back by 2pm").
- If you are working remotely, answer your texts and emails promptly, and make sure your calls are forwarded to a phone that you can answer within two rings.

THE QUICKEST WAY TO GET FIRED: INSUBORDINATION

In school, you are mostly judged on your individual accomplishments relative to some objective standard. Skipping an assignment isn't fatal. Maybe your grade will take a hit but missing one deadline won't generally get you kicked out of school.

The workplace is different. At work, it's not about your wonderful, original achievements. It's about keeping systems running and customers happy. Your responsibilities might not make sense to you, and the company's processes might seem antiquated. But this is not the time to show off your brilliance by telling your bosses how stupid their way of doing things is.

At work, refusing an assignment isn't like skipping a reflection paper. You can get fired for not doing what your boss tells you to. It's called insubordination.

This may seem unfair. You were hired for your smarts. Organizations are full of inefficiencies, and it doesn't seem right that anyone, least of all yourself, should waste time on poorly designed processes or projects.

The problem is, it's not up to the new employee to decide how things get done. Maybe a few changes could make things more efficient or profitable. But if you suggest an improvement and your boss says, "Thanks for sharing, now do it the way I told you," do it the way your boss told you.

It may be that your bosses are greedy or incompetent. But if they are, you can be sure someone already knows about it and has decided not to do anything about it. Are you, the new hire, going to reform the entire system? A more benign possibility is that processes are the way they are because of laws, contracts, accreditation requirements, or legacy software.

If things really are bad—if you are being asked to do something illegal, or you're getting stuck with menial or low-visibility jobs while your co-workers get the plum assignments—then it's time to start looking for another job.

STAY OUT OF TROUBLE

Be kind, thoughtful, teachable, and adaptable. Before you say anything, ask yourself: *Could this make me look like a know-it-all, a bigot, or that person who thinks the rules don't apply to me?* Be very careful about putting things in writing, especially jokes. Without nonverbal cues, a written message that was meant as light-hearted or sarcastic can come off as offensive.

Except for handshakes, don't initiate touching anyone. Some people or cultures are more "huggy" than others, so you should accept hugs if they're part of the normal workplace interaction.

Your co-workers may try to recruit you into taking sides in an ongoing feud. Don't let yourself get pulled in. If someone is breaking the law or doing something egregious, report it quietly and anonymously to law enforcement and/or HR. If what they are doing is not dangerous or destructive to others, stay out of it.

Avoid political discussions at work. If someone tries to draw you into a debate, resist the temptation to point out how wrong they are. Smile politely, claim you do not know much about the issue, and be on your way as quickly as you can.

Somewhere offsite, document all the good things that you have done so you can include them in future resumes and cover letters and remind your boss of them shortly before review time.

You should also document instances of discrimination, harassment, or illegal or unethical activity—including names, dates, location, and possible witnesses—in the unfortunate event that you might have to make a complaint or consult a lawyer.

AVOID BLATANT PERSONAL PHONE USE DURING WORK HOURS.

Employers complain about new hires who can't stay off their phones. Reserve texting, checking email, or playing a game for when you're not in the company of your boss or colleagues. Search "fired for texting" to get an idea of how people are discussing this issue.

NO, YOU CAN'T BE AN ASTRONAUT

10

WHAT ABOUT REMOTE WORK?

Remote work is not new. However the onset of the COVID-19 pandemic forced employers to transition quickly and on a mass scale to online work. Many of those with little previous experience of remote work found that they preferred working from home, avoiding commute time and contagion [118]. Part-time workers and those with longer commutes are especially keen to continue working from home [119].

Some employers have embraced remote work to an extent, taking advantage of reduced real estate costs and a wider pool of worker talent. However, companies and executives in the United States are more eager about returning to work than most employees are [120, 121]. A 2021 survey found that three-quarters of executives reported a desire to return to the office three to five days per week, while only one quarter of employees did [122]. Managing a remote team can be tricky, remote work can introduce security risks, and some employers do not trust employees to do their jobs unsupervised.

It's not just employers who are interested in getting workers back into the office. As more and more employees are able to work from home or other remote locations, there may be less demand for office space, which could lead to lower rental rates and reduced income for commercial real estate developers and landlords.

For experienced workers who already have a strong personal and professional network, remote work can be a good choice. It offers the ability to work from anywhere, reduced commuting time, and greater work-life balance. Some workers can get more done when they are able to work in a comfortable and distraction-free environment.

Junior-level workers who work remotely can feel excluded from networks and may get passed over for opportunities if they are not already well-known in the company. Some may find that working remotely can be isolating, as they do not have the same opportunities for face-to-face interaction with their colleagues. Communication can be more challenging in a remote work environment, as remote employees may not have the same access to real-time information or informal interaction as those who are on site. There's no online equivalent of spontaneously grabbing a cup of coffee with a colleague.

From the point of view of building your career, your best bet is to make yourself available for at least part-time in-person work. Interpersonal interaction on the job can enable you to network in a way that remote work cannot.

If you do accept a completely remote position, make sure you have robust internet access, and be prepared to find a new position on short notice. Your employer is probably already figuring out how to move your remote position to a lower cost of living area, or even overseas, in order to be able to pay less.

11

A GOOD LIFE, NOT A DREAM JOB

You don't have to abandon your dreams. But you should let go of the idea that there is only one dream job out there that will make you happy. The idea that you have to be SO PASSIONATE ABOUT YOUR JOB THAT YOU NEVER EVEN WANT TO GO HOME AT NIGHT is a destructive myth that makes people feel inadequate and guilty [123].

Even dream jobs have their not-so-dreamy parts. Writers deal with mean reviews [124], an unsteady publishing industry [125], and an indifferent reading public [126]. Athletes risk life-changing, irreversible injuries [127]. Astronauts have to prepare for zero gravity in a whirling contraption nicknamed the Vomit Comet [128].

Jim Bird of WorkLifeBalance.com says you don't have to be passionate about your job, but you can take pleasure in doing a great job. And you can derive fulfillment from other parts of your life, like your family, friends, pets, hobbies, and creative endeavors.

WILL YOU EVER BE HAPPY?

How do you feel about the following:

1. Your city
2. Your residence

3. The neighbors you have
4. The high school you attended
5. The climate where you live
6. The movies produced today
7. The quality of food you buy
8. Today's cars
9. The local paper
10. Your relaxation time
11. Your first name
12. The people you know
13. Television programs
14. Local speed limits
15. The way people drive
16. Advertising
17. The way you were raised
18. Phone service
19. Public transportation
20. Restaurant food
21. Yourself
22. Modern art
23. Popular music
24. $8\frac{1}{2}$ x 11 paper
25. Your telephone number

This list is called the Neutral Objects Satisfaction Questionnaire. Studies show that people who are generally satisfied with the objects listed above are also likely to be satisfied with their jobs, while those who are dissatisfied with everything around them also tend to be dissatisfied with their work [129].

Your job does matter, of course. A great job can boost your well-being, and a miserable workplace can make your life feel like a chore. But people do seem to have a baseline level of happiness. Happiness in adolescence is a good predictor of happiness in adulthood [130] and much of baseline happiness is inherited (if you're a natural grump, that's one more thing you can blame on your parents)

[131]. Aside from your DNA, factors influencing your happiness include your circumstances and your "happiness-relevant activities and practices"[132].

Here are some tips you can use to increase your happiness and well-being:

- Engage in kindness and gratitude. Some ways you can do this are writing letters expressing gratitude, counting your blessings, and performing acts of kindness for others [132].
- Spend time outdoors [133].
- Get physical exercise [134].
- Get enough sleep. Arrange your sleep hours so you wake up naturally, without needing an alarm [56, 135-137]
- Spend time with your friends and family. A good social life brings as much happiness as an extra $130,000 per year [138-140].
- Quit smoking and get regular check-ups. Good health is worth nearly half a million dollars a year in happiness [139].
- While some people enjoy driving, commuting can be stressful [141, 142]; it might be worth it to spend the extra money to move closer to your workplace.
- Keep your home and your workspace neat enough that you can find what you need when you need it. Clutter can lead to the unpleasant sense that your house isn't really your home [143, 144]

These practices, combined with a job you can stand, can add up to a nice life. You may even have enough spare time to...try out your dreams.

TAKE YOUR DREAM UP FOR A TEST FLIGHT

Kristen Ridout quit her administrative job to pursue broadcast journalism.

She started in small, remote markets and moved often. But the economics of the industry caught up with her.

"While I commuted 45 minutes along mountainous roads at four in the morning to report the news, the opportunities for raises and promotions faded away. Two years of doing everything I could to move up in the company were proving fruitless."

She changed industries when pursuing her dream was no longer sustainable.

"I don't regret following my dreams to become a journalist, because I would have been unhappy had I not given it a try. I also don't regret throwing in the towel after five years, because I tried my best." [145]

Sometimes your dreams are based on incomplete information. You may have dreamed of living in a big city, but once you get there, you find you can't stand the noise, crowds, and high cost of living. You may start your own business because you want to set your hours and be your own boss, only to find that you can't take a day off, it's impossible to find employees as dedicated as you are, and every one of your customers thinks they're your boss.

You can change course, and you can keep your dream career as a hobby. You might even enjoy it more without the pressure of trying to make it cover your living expenses. Many people have ordinary day jobs and in their nonwork time enjoy singing, playing music, acting, or writing novels.

And once in a while, a hobby really can turn into a dream job.

Tess Gerritsen writes the bestselling Rizzoli & Isles medical thrillers. But she was a medical doctor first. Elle Boon, Jana DeLeon, and Joanna Penn all quit their corporate jobs to pursue successful writing careers. It can happen. But like Kristen Ridout, you have to set your limits, and know when to quit.

You don't have to choose between throwing aside money and security to pursue your passion versus grinding away at a soul-sucking desk job. You can choose to build financial security, which will give you the freedom to pursue your dreams on the side. Only you can decide how much security you need, how much risk you can live with, and how you want to spend your time and your life. If you're married or partnered, and one of you is pursuing a long-shot career (novelist, entrepreneur, tenure-track humanities professor), you must listen to each other, stay informed, keep talking, and go to counseling if necessary.

Take care of your body; it's the life-support system for your brain.

Reject envy; appreciate the talents of others as a gift to the world. This is harder than it may seem. Our consumer economy depends on covetousness and discontent [146]. But as much as you can, adopt the attitude of a sports fan, whose pleasure in an athlete's achievement is unmarred by jealousy. Enjoy watching a spacewalk even if you're not the one floating hundreds of miles above the earth.

Kindness is crucial. Be good to those around you and kind to yourself. Invest in activities and attitudes that will keep you too engaged to have time to envy others and will bring you satisfaction in the long run.

REFERENCES

1. Cappelli, P.H., *Skill gaps, skill shortages, and skill mismatches: Evidence and arguments for the United States.* ILR Review, 2015. **68**(2): p. 251-290.
2. Xue, Y. and R.C. Larson, *STEM crisis or STEM surplus? Yes and yes.* Monthly labor review, 2015. **2015**.
3. Charette, R.N., *The STEM crisis is a myth.* IEEE Spectrum, 2013. **50**(9): p. 44-59.
4. Platform, N.L., N.Q. Polls, and J. Market, *The positive implications of internships on early career outcomes.* NACE Journal, 2017.
5. Giorgio, D.P., E. Commission, and IZA, *Studying abroad and earnings: A meta-analysis.* Journal of Economic Surveys, 2022. **36**(4): p. 1096-1129.
6. Kiefer, C., et al., *Predictive Characteristics of Adequate Employment in Baccalaureate-Prepared Graduates.* Impacting Education: Journal on Transforming Professional Practice, 2022. **7**(4): p. 26-32.
7. Federal Reserve Bank of New York. *The Labor Market for Recent College Graduates.* 2022[cited 2022 December 03]; Available from: https://web.archive.org/web/20221203232953/https://www.newyorkfed.org/research/college-labor-market/college-labor-market_compare-majors.html
8. Williams, J.C., et al., *Stable scheduling increases productivity and sales: The Stable Scheduling Study.* University of California Hastings College of the Law, University of Chicago School of Social Service Administration, University of California Kenan-Flagler Business School, 2018.
9. Lennon, C., *How Do Online Degrees Affect Labor Market Prospects? Evidence From A Correspondence Audit Study.* 2019.

REFERENCES

10. com, B.C.S.t.b., *The Bayer facts of science education XVI: US STEM workforce shortage—myth or reality? Fortune 1000 talent recruiters on the debate.* Journal of Science Education and Technology, 2014. **23**(5): p. 617-623.
11. Stevenson, H.J., *Myths and Motives behind STEM (Science, Technology, Engineering, and Mathematics) Education and the STEM-Worker Shortage Narrartive.* Issues in Teacher Education, 2014. **23**(1): p. 133-146.
12. Berghel, H., *STEM crazy.* Computer, 2015. **48**(9): p. 75-80.
13. Salzman, H. and B. Lieff Benderly, *STEM Performance and Supply: Assessing the Evidence for Education Policy.* Journal of Science Education and Technology, 2019. **28**(1): p. 9-25.
14. National Center for Education Statistics. *Rates of high school completion and bachelor's degree attainment among persons age 25 and over, by race/ethnicity and sex: Selected years, 1910 through 2021.* 2021; Available from: https://nces.ed.gov/programs/digest/d21/tables/dt21_104.10.asp.
15. Association of Public & Land-Grant Universities. *How does a college degree improve graduates' employment and earnings potential?* 2021 [cited 2021; Available from: https://www.aplu.org/projects-and-initiatives/college-costs-tuition-and-financial-aid/publicuvalues/employment-earnings.html.
16. Carnevale, A.P. and S.J. Rose, *The Undereducated American.* Georgetown University Center on Education and the Workforce, 2011.
17. Carnevale, A.P., N. Smith, and J. Strohl, *Help wanted: Projections of job and education requirements through 2018.* 2010: Lumina Foundation.
18. Habibi, N. and A. Kamis, *Reaching for the stars and settling for the moon: recent trends in overeducation of US workers 2002-2016.* Journal of education and work, 2021. **34**(2): p. 143-157.
19. Barnichon, R. and Y. Zylberberg, *Underemployment and the Trickle-Down of Unemployment.* American Economic Journal: Macroeconomics, 2019. **11**(2): p. 40-78.
20. Morin, R., A. Brown, and R. Fry. *The Rising Cost of Not Going to College.* 2014 [cited 2022; Available from: https://www.pewresearch.org/social-trends/2014/02/11/the-rising-cost-of-not-going-to-college/.

21. Howell, D.R. and A.L. Kalleberg, *Declining job quality in the United States: Explanations and evidence.* RSF: The Russell Sage Foundation Journal of the Social Sciences, 2019. **5**(4): p. 1-53.
22. Bureau of Labor Statistics. *Occupations that Need More Education for Entry are Projected to Grow Faster Than Average.* 2022; Available from: https://www.bls.gov/emp/tables/education-summary.htm.
23. Stark, E. and P. Poppler, *What are they thinking? Employers requiring college degrees for low-skilled jobs.* SAM Advanced Management Journal, 2016. **81**(3): p. 17-27.
24. Dwyer, R.E. and E.O. Wright, *Low-wage job growth, polarization, and the limits and opportunities of the service economy.* RSF: The Russell Sage Foundation Journal of the Social Sciences, 2019. **5**(4): p. 56-76.
25. Bruenig, M., *Why Education Does Not Fix Poverty,* in *Policyshop.* 2015, Demos.
26. Harrington, P.E. and A.M. Sum, *College Labor Shortages in 2018?* New England Journal of Higher Education, 2010.
27. Hall, J.V. and A.B. Krueger, *An analysis of the labor market for Uber's driver-partners in the United States.* 2016, National Bureau of Economic Research.
28. Georgetown University Center on Education and the Workforce. *FAQs.* 2017 [cited 2017; Available from: https://cew.georgetown.edu/about-the-center/faqs/.
29. Lumina Foundation for Education, *Grant Database.* 2019.
30. Education, L.F.f. *Lumina's Goal.* 2019; Available from: https://www.luminafoundation.org/lumina-goal.
31. Loonin, D. and J.M. Morgan, *Aiming Higher: Looking Beyond Completion to Restore the Promise of Higher Education.* Journal of Law and Education, 2019. **48**(4): p. 423-448.
32. Rhoades, G., *The Incomplete Completion Agenda: Implications for Academe and the Academy.* Liberal Education, 2012. **98**(1): p. 18-25.
33. Horowitz, J., *Relative education and the advantage of a college degree.* American sociological review, 2018. **83**(4): p. 771-801.
34. Carlsson, F., O. Johansson-Stenman, and P. Martinsson, *Do you enjoy having more than others? Survey evidence of positional goods.* Economica,

2007. **74**(296): p. 586-598.
35. Webber, D.A., *Are college costs worth it? How ability, major, and debt affect the returns to schooling.* Economics of Education Review, 2016. **53**: p. 296-310.
36. Emmons, W.R., A.H. Kent, and L. Ricketts, *Is college still worth it? The new calculus of falling returns.* The New Calculus of Falling Returns, 2019: p. 297-329.
37. Huber, M.T., *Is College for Everyone?* Change: The Magazine of Higher Learning, 2017. **49**(1): p. 7-13.
38. Tigar, L. *The worst career advice, according to 6 life coaches*. theladders.com, 2017.
39. Flood, A., *Most writers earn less than £600 a year, survey reveals*, in The Guardian. 2014.
40. Farmer, A.S., *Student-Athlete to Professional Athlete: Confronting the Brutal Facts.*
41. Kerr-Dineen, L., *Here are your odds of becoming a professional athlete (they're not good)*, in USAToday.com. 2016.
42. Seedhouse, E., *Prepare for Launch: The Astronaut Training Process.* 2018: Springer Science & Business Media.
43. Mann, A., *Your Odds of Becoming an Astronaut Are Going Up*, in Wired. 2013, Conde Nast.
44. onlinecasino.ca. *The Odds of Success.* 2017; Available from: https://www.onlinecasino.ca/odds-of-success.
45. Holland, J.L., *Exploring careers with a typology: What we have learned and some new directions.* American Psychologist, 1996. **51**(4): p. 397.
46. Hoff, K.A., et al., *Interest fit and job satisfaction: A systematic review and meta-analysis.* Journal of Vocational Behavior, 2020: p. 103503.
47. Rode, J.C., et al., *A time-lagged study of emotional intelligence and salary.* Journal of Vocational Behavior, 2017. **101**: p. 77-89.
48. Song, L.J., et al., *The differential effects of general mental ability and emotional intelligence on academic performance and social interactions.* Intelligence, 2010. **38**(1): p. 137-143.
49. Cote, S. and C.T. Miners, *Emotional intelligence, cognitive intelligence, and*

50. Baron-Cohen, S. *Mind in the Eyes Test*. 2021 [cited 2021 May 1]; Available from: http://socialintelligence.labinthewild.org/mite/.
51. Kim, H., et al., *Multiracial Reading the Mind in the Eyes Test (MRMET): an inclusive version of an influential measure.* 2022.
52. Open Source Psychometrics Project. *Personality-Based Emotional Intelligence Test.* 2021[cited 2021 May 1]; Available from: https://openpsychometrics.org/tests/EI.php.
53. Roberts, R.D., R. Schulze, and C. MacCann, *The measurement of emotional intelligence: A decade of progress.* The Sage handbook of personality theory and assessment, 2008. **2**: p. 461-482.
54. Wilkins, M.M., *Signs That You Lack Emotional Intelligence*, in Harvard Business Review. 2014.
55. Killgore, W.D., et al., *Emotional intelligence is associated with connectivity within and between resting state networks.* Social Cognitive and Affective Neuroscience, 2017. **12**(10): p. 1624-1636.
56. Killgore, W.D., *Self-reported sleep correlates with prefrontal-amygdala functional connectivity and emotional functioning.* Sleep, 2013. **36**(11): p. 1597-1608.
57. Pescuric, A. and W.C. Byham, *The new look of behavior modeling.* Training & Development, 1996. **50**(7): p. 24-31.
58. Nafukho, F.M., et al., *Developing Emotional Intelligence Skills among Practicing Leaders: Reality or Myth?* Performance Improvement Quarterly, 2016. **29**(1): p. 71-87.
59. Myers, I.B., *Introduction to type®*. 1998: CPP.
60. King, S.P. and B.A. Mason, *Myers-Briggs Type Indicator.* The Wiley Encyclopedia of Personality and Individual Differences: Measurement and Assessment, 2020: p. 315-319.
61. Grant, A., *MBTI, If You Want Me Back, You Need to Change Too*, in Medium. 2015.
62. Stein, R. and A.B. Swan, *Evaluating the validity of Myers-Briggs Type Indicator theory: A teaching tool and window into intuitive psychology.* Social and Personality Psychology Compass, 2019. **13**(2): p. e12434.

63. Soto, C.J., *Paradigm Shitt I to the Integrative Big Five Trait Taxonomy.*
64. Larson, L.M., P.J. Rottinghaus, and F.H. Borgen, *Meta-analyses of Big Six interests and Big Five personality factors.* Journal of Vocational Behavior, 2002. **61**(2): p. 217-239.
65. Pittenger, D.J., *Cautionary Comments Regarding the Myers-Briggs Type Indicator.* Consulting Psychology Journal: Practice & Research, 2005. **57**(2): p. 210-221.
66. Hughes, D.J., et al., *Using personality questionnaires for selection.* The Wiley Blackwell handbook of the psychology of recruitment, selection & retention. Chichester: Wiley-Blackwell, 2017.
67. Saunders, F.W., *Katharine and Isabel: Mother's light, daughter's journey.* 1991: Nicholas Brealey Publishing.
68. John, O.P. and S. Srivastava, *The Big Five trait taxonomy: History, measurement, and theoretical perspectives.*, in *Handbook of personality: Theory and research*, L.A. Pervin and O.P. John, Editors. 1999, Guilford Press: New York. p. 102–138.
69. Culp, G. and A. Smith, *Understanding psychological type to improve project team performance.* Journal of Management in Engineering, 2001. **17**(1): p. 24-33.
70. De Frum, F., *Personality and interests as predictors of educational streaming and achievement.* 1996.
71. Gale, C.R., et al., *When is higher neuroticism protective against death? Findings from UK Biobank.* Psychological science, 2017. **28**(9): p. 1345-1357.
72. Martin, C.C., *Healthier Without Knowing It: Healthy Neuroticism Does Not Predict Self-Rated Health.* 2016.
73. Perkins, A.M. and P.J. Corr, *Can worriers be winners? The association between worrying and job performance.* Personality and Individual Differences, 2005. **38**(1): p. 25-31.
74. Avis, J.M., J.D. Kudisch, and V.J. Fortunato, *Examining the incremental validity and adverse impact of cognitive ability and conscientiousness on job performance.* Journal of Business and Psychology, 2002. **17**(1): p. 87-105.
75. Barrick, M.R. and M.K. Mount, *Select on conscientiousness and emotional*

stability, in *Handbook of Principles of Organizational Behavior*, E.A. Locke, Editor. 2004, Blackwell: Malden, MA. p. 15-28.
76. Borman, W.C., et al., *Personality Predictors of Citizenship Performance.* International Journal of Selection and Assessment, 2001. **9**(1-2): p. 52-69.
77. Boyce, C.J., A.M. Wood, and G.D.A. Brown, *The dark side of conscientiousness: Conscientious people experience greater drops in life satisfaction following unemployment.* Journal of Research in Personality, 2010. **44**(4): p. 535-539.
78. Dahm, A.-S., et al., *The burden of conscientiousness? Examining brain activation and cortisol response during social evaluative stress.* Psychoneuroendocrinology, 2017. **78**(Supplement C): p. 48-56.
79. Carnevale, A.P., et al., *Major matters most: The economic value of bachelor's degrees from the University of Texas System.* 2017.
80. Eide, E.R., M.J. Hilmer, and M.H. Showalter, *Is it where you go or what you study? The relative influence of college selectivity and college major on earnings.* Contemporary Economic Policy, 2016. **34**(1): p. 37-46.
81. Witteveen, D. and P. Attewell, *The earnings payoff from attending a selective college.* Social Science Research, 2017. **66**: p. 154-169.
82. Walsemann, K.M., B.A. Bell, and R.A. Hummer, *Effects of Timing and Level of Degree Attained on Depressive Symptoms and Self-Rated Health at Midlife.* American Journal of Public Health, 2012. **102**(3): p. 557-563.
83. Ma, J., et al., *State-level educational disparities in mortality in the United States, 2010-2014.* Preventive medicine, 2017.
84. Ma, J., M. Pender, and M. Welch, *Education Pays 2019: The Benefits of Higher Education for Individuals and Society. Trends in Higher Education Series*, in *Trends in Higher Education*, C. Board, Editor. 2019.
85. Choi, S., *When everyone goes to college: The causal effect of college expansion on earnings.* Social Science Research, 2015. **50**: p. 229-245.
86. Government Accountability Office, *LOW-WAGE WORKERS: Poverty and Use of Selected Federal Social Safety Net Programs Persist among Working Families.* 2017.
87. Ost, B., W. Pan, and D.A. Webber, *The Returns to College Persistence*

for Marginal Students: Regression Discontinuity Evidence from University Dismissal Policies. 2016.

88. Giani, M.S., P. Attewell, and D. Walling, *The Value of an Incomplete Degree: Heterogeneity in the Labor Market Benefits of College Non-Completion.* The Journal of Higher Education, 2019: p. 1-26.

89. Webber, D.A., *Projected Lifetime Earnings for Bachelor's Degree Holders by Major.* Chemical Engineering, 2018. **3**(2,861,315): p. 4,138,457.

90. Hein, V., B. Smerdon, and M. Sambolt, *Predictors of Postsecondary Success.* College and Career Readiness and Success Center, 2013.

91. Bartik, T.J. and B. Hershbein, *Degrees of poverty: The relationship between family income background and the returns to education.* 2018.

92. Abel, J.R. and R. Deitz, *College may not pay off for everyone.* Liberty Street Economics, Federal Reserve Bank of New York, 2014.

93. Hersh, R.H., *Intention and Perceptions A National Survey of Public Attitudes Toward Liberal Arts Education.* Change: The Magazine of Higher Learning, 1997. **29**(2): p. 16-23.

94. Bradforth, S.E., et al., *University learning: Improve undergraduate science education.* Nature News, 2015. **523**(7560): p. 282.

95. Bettinger, E.P. and B.T. Long, *Mass Instruction or Higher Learning? The Impact of College Class Size on Student Retention and Graduation.* Education Finance and Policy, 2016.

96. Bandiera, O., V. Larcinese, and I. Rasul, *Heterogeneous Class Size Effects: New Evidence from a Panel of University Students*.* The Economic Journal, 2010. **120**(549): p. 1365-1398.

97. Cuseo, J., *The empirical case against large class size: adverse effects on the teaching, learning, and retention of first-year students.* The Journal of Faculty Development, 2007. **21**(1): p. 5-21.

98. De Paola, M. and V. Scoppa, *The effects of class size on the achievement of college students.* The Manchester School, 2011. **79**(6): p. 1061-1079.

99. Johnson, I., *Class Size and Student Performance at a Public Research University: A Cross-Classified Model.* Research in Higher Education, 2010. **51**(8): p. 701-723.

100. Kokkelenberg, E.C., M. Dillon, and S.M. Christy, *The effects of class size*

on student grades at a public university. Economics of Education Review, 2008. **27**(2): p. 221-233.
101. Kara, E., M. Tonin, and M. Vlassopoulos, *Class size effects in higher education: differences across STEM and non-STEM fields.* Economics of Education Review, 2021. **82**: p. 102104.
102. Armona, L., R. Chakrabarti, and M. Lovenheim, *How does for-profit college attendance affect student loans, defaults, and earnings?* 2017.
103. Cellini, S.R. and N. Turner, *Gainfully Employed? Assessing the Employment and Earnings of For-Profit College Students Using Administrative Data.* 2016, National Bureau of Economic Research.
104. Scott-Clayton, J., *What Accounts for Gaps in Student Loan Default, and What Happens After. Evidence Speaks Reports, Vol 2,# 57.* Center on Children and Families at Brookings, 2017.
105. Iuliano, J., *The Student Loan Bankruptcy Gap.* 2020.
106. Rivera, L.A., *Pedigree: How elite students get elite jobs.* 2016: Princeton University Press.
107. Bruni, F., *Where You Go Is Not Who You'll Be: An Antidote to the College Admissions Mania.* 2015: Grand Central Publishing.
108. Executive Office of the President of the United States, *USING FEDERAL DATA TO MEASURE AND IMPROVE THE PERFORMANCE OF U.S. INSTITUTIONS OF HIGHER EDUCATION.* 2017.
109. Ray, J. and S. Kafka, *Life in college matters for life after college.* Life, 2014. **5**.
110. Silva, E. and T. White, *The Carnegie unit: Past, present, and future.* Change: The Magazine of Higher Learning, 2015. **47**(2): p. 68-72.
111. Warren, C., *10 People Who Lost Jobs Over Social Media Mistakes,* in *Mashable.com.* 2011.
112. Drouin, M., et al., *Facebook fired: Legal perspectives and young adults' opinions on the use of social media in hiring and firing decisions.* Computers in Human Behavior, 2015. **46**: p. 123-128.
113. *Elonis v. US,* in *S. Ct.* 2015, Supreme Court. p. 2001.
114. Curran, D., *Are you ready? Here is all the data Facebook and Google have on you.* The Guardian, 2018. **30**.

115. Lucas, S., *10 ways school is different than the working world*, in *MoneyWatch*. 2014, CBS News.
116. Gaines, J., *Women in Male-Dominated Careers*. Women, 2017. **5**: p. 3-2017.
117. Yam, K.C., R. Fehr, and C.M. Barnes, *Morning employees are perceived as better employees: Employees' start times influence supervisor performance ratings.* Journal of Applied Psychology, 2014. **99**(6): p. 1288-1299.
118. Barrero, J.M., N. Bloom, and S.J. Davis, *Why working from home will stick.* 2021, National Bureau of Economic Research.
119. Appel-Meulenbroek, R., et al., *How to attract employees back to the office? A stated choice study on hybrid working preferences.* Journal of Environmental Psychology, 2022. **81**: p. 101784.
120. Barrero, J.M., N. Bloom, and S.J. Davis, *Let me work from home, or I will find another job.* University of Chicago, Becker Friedman Institute for Economics Working Paper, 2021(2021-87).
121. Sherman, A., *Making sense of why executives are eager to get employees back in the office*, in *CNBC*. 2022.
122. Future Forum, in *Future Forum Pulse,*. 2021.
123. Levy, J., *The Dream Job Is a Myth. Focus Instead on Living Your Best Life.*, in *Entrepreneur*. 2017.
124. *One-Star Book Reviews*. 2017; Available from: http://onestarbookreview.tumblr.com/.
125. Horne, A., *Publishing: the last (and next?) five years.* The Indexer, 2017. **35**(1): p. 2-9.
126. Perrin, A., *Who doesn't read books in America?* Pew Research Center. 2019.
127. Iverson, G.L., *Chronic traumatic encephalopathy and risk of suicide in former athletes.* Br J Sports Med, 2014. **48**(2): p. 162-164.
128. Dempsey, R., et al., *Thank you for flying the vomit comet.* The Physics Teacher, 2007. **45**(2): p. 75-79.
129. Judge, T.A. and C.L. Hulin, *Job satisfaction as a reflection of disposition: A multiple source causal analysis.* Organizational Behavior and Human Decision Processes, 1993. **56**(3): p. 388-421.
130. Staw, B., N. E. Bell, and J. A. Clausen, *The Dispositional Approach To Job Attitudes: A Lifetime Longitudinal Test*. Vol. 31. 1986. 56.

131. Røysamb, E., et al., *Genetics, personality and wellbeing. A twin study of traits, facets and life satisfaction.* Scientific Reports, 2018. **8**(1): p. 1-13.
132. Lyubomirsky, S., K.M. Sheldon, and D. Schkade, *Pursuing happiness: The architecture of sustainable change.* Review of general psychology, 2005. **9**(2): p. 111.
133. MacKerron, G. and S. Mourato, *Happiness is greater in natural environments.* Global Environmental Change, 2013. **23**(5): p. 992-1000.
134. Lubans, D., et al., *Physical activity for cognitive and mental health in youth: A systematic review of mechanisms.* Pediatrics, 2016: p. e20161642.
135. Kripke, D.F., et al., *Mortality associated with sleep duration and insomnia.* Archives of general psychiatry, 2002. **59**(2): p. 131-136.
136. Ong, A.D., et al., *Positive affect and sleep: A systematic review.* Sleep medicine reviews, 2017. **35**: p. 21-32.
137. Lieberman, H.R., et al., *Severe decrements in cognition function and mood induced by sleep loss, heat, dehydration, and undernutrition during simulated combat.* Biological psychiatry, 2005. **57**(4): p. 422-429.
138. Powdthavee, N., *How much does money really matter? Estimating the causal effects of income on happiness.* Empirical economics, 2010. **39**(1): p. 77-92.
139. Powdthavee, N., *Putting a price tag on friends, relatives, and neighbours: Using surveys of life satisfaction to value social relationships.* The Journal of Socio-Economics, 2008. **37**(4): p. 1459-1480.
140. Leung, A., et al., *Searching for happiness: The importance of social capital.* Journal of Happiness Studies, 2011. **12**(3): p. 443-462.
141. Ding, D., et al., *Driving: a road to unhealthy lifestyles and poor health outcomes.* PloS one, 2014. **9**(6): p. e94602.
142. Novaco, R.W. and O.I. Gonzalez, *Commuting and well-being.* Technology and well-being, 2009. **3**: p. 174-4.
143. Rogers, C.J. and R. Hart, *Home and the extended-self: Exploring associations between clutter and wellbeing.* Journal of Environmental Psychology, 2021. **73**: p. 101553.
144. Roster, C.A., J.R. Ferrari, and M.P. Jurkat, *The dark side of home: Assessing possession 'clutter' on subjective well-being.* Journal of Environmental Psychology, 2016. **46**: p. 32-41.

145. Ridout, K., *Reality Check: I Left My Dream Job To Be More Practical*, in *Entrepreneur.com*. 2015, Entrepreneur Media.
146. Wooten, D.B., R.L. Harrison, and N. Mitchell, *Benign envy: is there a dark side of light green?* AMS review, 2011. **1**(3-4): p. 137-139.

FURTHER READING

Amabile, T., & Kramer, S. (2011). The progress principle: Using small wins to ignite joy, engagement, and creativity at work. Harvard Business Press.

Barry, D. (1986). Claw Your Way to the Top: How to Become the Head of a Major Corporation in Roughly a Week. Rodale.

Cappelli, P. (2012). Why good people can't get jobs: The skills gap and what companies can do about it. University of Pennsylvania Press.

Carnegie, D. (1981). How to win friends and influence people. Simon and Schuster.

Ehrenreich, B. (2010). Nickel and dimed: On (not) getting by in America. Metropolitan Books.

Groening, M. (1987). Work is hell: a cartoon book. WH Allen.

Reardon, K. K. (2002). The secret handshake: Mastering the politics of the business inner circle. Broadway Business.

Sutton, R. I. (2007). The no asshole rule: Building a civilized workplace and surviving one that isn't. Hachette UK.

ABOUT THE AUTHOR

Patience Fairweather is the pen name of a business school dean in the United States. Dr. Fairweather has nothing against people following their dreams, as long as they know what they're getting into. Find quick links to the online resources at **noyoucantbeanastronaut.com**.

www.ingramcontent.com/pod-product-compliance
Lightning Source LLC
Chambersburg PA
CBHW052116110526
44592CB00013B/1636